70

TIMES

7

70

TIMES

7

DANIEL'S MYSTERIOUS COUNTDOWN

AND

THE CHURCH'S HEROIC FUTURE

by

Nelson Walters

Ready For Jesus Publications (Wilmington, NC, 2018)
ISBN-13: 978-0692070925
ISBN-10: 0692070923

CONTENTS

ILLUSTRATIONS

A number of illustrations by 19th Century artist, Gustave Dore, are found within pages of this book. During his lifetime, Dore produced wood-cut illustrations that have graced the pages of Bibles throughout the last two centuries. You may have encountered them. Dore contributed to the genre` by incorporating a life-like quality to his depictions of Bible accounts not often found in previous illustrations.

CONTACT

The Gospel in the End Times Ministries

www.TheGospelInTheEndTimes.com

nelson@thegospelintheendtimes.com

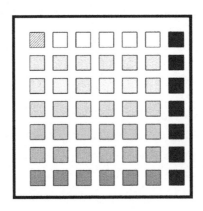

PART ONE:

SIGNIFICANCE AND MYSTERY

Chapter One

HUMBLE HANDS

*"I delivered to you as of **first importance** what I also received ..."*

(1 Cor. 15:3 NASB)

What is the most significant prophecy in the Bible? Was it the first prophecy, Gen. 3:15, when God promised to undo man's fall into sin by crushing the head of the serpent? Was it the last prophecy, Rev. 22:1-5, in which the Apostle John describes his revelation of our final "heavenly home" where we will dwell with Jesus and the Father forever? An argument could certainly be made for these and dozens of other prophecies. All of God's Word is significant!

But there is an ancient prophecy found in the Book of Daniel that foretells both the First and Second Coming of our Messiah, Jesus. It gives us a countdown or a timetable upon which to calculate those comings. Its breadth spans 2500 years, from Daniel to our present day, and beyond. Certainly, a very strong argument can be made that *this* prophecy, known in our Christian culture as "the *70 Weeks Prophecy*," is *the* most significant of all.

Christian scholars from all corners of the prophetic spectrum agree on the central importance of this prophecy:

One might well argue that Daniel 9:24-27 is both the most complex and the most crucial text in either testament bearing on the subject of biblical prophecy. — Sam Storms[1]

The interpretation of the revelation given to Daniel concerning the seventy weeks (Dan. 9:24-27) constitutes one of the determining factors in the whole system of prophecy. — John Walvoord[2]

No two prophecy experts could be further apart in their eschatological beliefs: the amillennialist, Storms, and the dispensationalist, Walvoord. But they both agree on the central importance of the *70 Weeks Prophecy*.

If this truly is the *most* significant prophecy in the Bible, then it stands to reason that it should also be the best understood prophecy. One would imagine that countless generations of scholars would have studied it and come to a unanimous agreement as to its meaning. However, that is simply not the case. Although scholars throughout the ages have diligently studied it, there is little or no agreement about its meaning. In fact, the starting point of the countdown, the ending point, and nearly every word and concept found in between are sources of disagreement.

I suspect that this disagreement may be part of the reason you purchased this book. And it's that same disagreement and the *mystery* of this prophecy that led me to dig deeply into this subject matter. If this prophecy

---

[1] "Daniel's 70 Weeks," *Sam Storms*, last modified unknown, accessed February 3, 2018, http://samstorms.com/all-articles/post/daniels-70-weeks

[2] "The Seventieth Week of Daniel," Bible.org, last modified unknown, accessed February 3, 2018, https://bible.org/seriespage/chapter-5-seventieth-week-daniel

is the framework upon which all of our eschatological understanding is based, as mentioned by Dr. Walvoord, then we need to uncover and resolve as much of the mystery as possible.

THE MYSTERY OF SILENCE

The prophecy is rather unique. Given its importance, you would imagine that the Old Testament prophets and the writers of the Epistles would have each made reference to it, especially because it is the only prophecy that reveals the *timing* of the First Coming of Jesus. We can almost imagine the Apostle Paul writing:

> "But when the first 69 weeks were accomplished, God
> sent forth his son . . ." (fabricated quote of Paul)

But that is not what the Apostle said. He wrote, "*But when the **fullness of time had come**, God sent forth his Son*" (Gal. 4:4 ESV). In fact, Paul, Peter, John, and James never refer to these "weeks" mentioned by the prophet Daniel. The New Testament Epistles are **completely silent** on the "weeks." Not only are the Epistles silent on this prophecy, but the other Old Testament prophets never refer to these mysterious 70 Weeks either.

You and I must ask why that is. If the *70 Weeks Prophecy* is the most important prophecy in the Bible, what could have been God's purpose for excluding it from being at least referenced elsewhere in the Old Testament and in the Epistles? I mean, if I were living at the time of Peter and Paul, it would have been my "go-to" prophecy to prove that Jesus was the Messiah.

Interestingly, after the death and resurrection of Jesus, the ancient rabbis pronounced a curse on all those who attempted to calculate the timing of the coming of Messiah based on the *70 Weeks Prophecy*:

> A Sage said: "May the curse of heaven fall upon those who calculate the date of the advent of the Messiah, and thus create political and social unrest among the people."
> — Sanhedrin, 97b[3]

> Some of our Rabbis, in a further attempt to keep us from Daniel, even state that Daniel was wrong. — Alfred Edersheim[4]

The rabbis probably feared that the 69 "weeks" of the prophecy had already past and that the *70 Weeks Prophecy* was a direct link to — and proof of — the Messiahship of Jesus. It was likely for this reason that they forbade the calculation of the First Coming. In Chapter Six, we'll discover that even the Jewish calendar was altered to avoid the obvious link between the *70 Weeks Prophecy* and its fulfillment in Jesus.

The apostles would have known of this concern of the Jewish authorities and realized the powerful tool that a fully realized prophecy like this would have been in the first century. However, Peter, who spoke the first sermon on Pentecost, never referred to it. John, who wrote the Book

---

[3] Louis Newman and Samuel Spitz, *The Talmudic anthology: tales and teachings of the rabbis* (Behrman House, 1945): 277. ISBN 0874413036, 9780874413038
[4] Alfred Edersheim, *The Life and Times of Jesus The Messiah* (Peabody, MA: Hendrickson Publishers, 2000), p. 957

of Revelation, which contains over 500 known references to the Old Testament, doesn't refer to this amazing prophecy one time. This is especially significant, because most Christians believe the Book of Revelation is the Bible's best account of the "Tribulation," or the seven-year period of time derived from the *70 Weeks Prophecy* — the 70th Week of Daniel!

I have to conclude from this analysis that the *70 Weeks Prophecy* is **intentionally** absent from the Epistles and the Book of Revelation. And I must therefore assume that God didn't want it fully explained at that point in time. None of us knows the mind of God, and any attempt to discern why the Lord did not inspire the writers of the Epistles to refer to the *70 Weeks Prophecy* is pure conjecture. However, we must try.

POSSIBLE REASONS THE *70 WEEKS PROPHECY* IS NOT FOUND IN THE EPISTLES

We know from Scripture that God has partially hardened the hearts of the Jewish remnant until the "fullness of the gentiles has come in" (Rom. 11:25). Is it possible that this is one reason the prophecy remains an enigma? If the prophecy had been fully revealed and explained by the Apostles in the first century, Jews may have been cut to the core by its truth and come to faith in Jesus. Might the lack of clarity about this prophecy be one factor causing this partial hardening to continue? Perhaps, it is. In future chapters, we will discuss this lack of clarity in even greater detail.

It is also possible that God has kept various aspects of the prophecy regarding the final Tribulation — more properly known as the 70th Week of Daniel — from being disclosed until they are "needed." Two thousand years have lapsed since the resurrection of Jesus. In all those passing generations, there was no real need for a full disclosure of what that time period would entail. It may have been intriguing to our forefathers in the faith; but they didn't *need* that information to overcome the trials of their own lives.

Now, however, a generation is coming that may well need that information. In my opinion, it is entirely likely that, at the right moment, God will reveal to us exactly what the entire prophecy means. This could be the generation for that revelation.

Regardless of what reason God has for not fully revealing what the *70 Weeks Prophecy* means, the lack of explanation in both the Epistles and the Old Testament has led to great confusion and speculation. Numerous traditions — unbiblical interpretations — have sprung up within the Church. I used to believe in some of these and perhaps you currently still do. For this reason, I ask that you hold your opinions of the *70 Weeks Prophecy* loosely, in humble hands. Because perhaps the time has come for some of the mystery to be revealed. Amazing new revelations about Israel's past and about the future destiny of the Church are contained in subsequent chapters. I invite you to join me on this journey of discovery.

Two of the questions that we will attempt to answer in this book dominate our thinking as we prepare for the return of Jesus:

Has the *70 Weeks Prophecy* been entirely fulfilled, or does a "70th Week of Daniel" still lie in the future?

This may be the central question addressed in this book. Throughout the ages, Christians have lined up on the two sides of this question, as "historicists" or "futurists." Every sentence of every verse of the *70 Weeks Prophecy* contributes understanding to this issue. After you complete the book, I sincerely believe that the answer to this question will be clear to you.

What is the Covenant with the Many found in Dan. 9:27?

A mysterious "he" confirms or strengthens a covenant for the entire 70th Week of this prophecy. Christians have offered many guesses as to what this verse means — from a strengthening of the Mosaic Covenant to the Antichrist making a peace treaty with Israel.

But is it possible that this passage actually contains a clue to a future that is more exciting, more heroic, and more glorious than anything the Church has ever imagined? We will begin to discuss this possibility in Chapter Eight.

There are a number of other stirring questions prompted by Daniel 9, the chapter that contains the 70th Week Prophecy. The following are only a sampling of the questions that we'll try to answer:

- What is the unexpected identity of the Prince who is to come?
- Is the Covenant with the Many something other than a peace treaty?
- Is there a new and "precise" solution to the countdown to the First Coming of Jesus?
- Do the 70 Weeks provide us with an accurate list of ancient Jubilee years and Shmitah years?
- Do the *Dead Sea Scrolls* provides us with a clear understanding of what first century Jews thought about the prophecy?

- Does the prophecy foretell a glorious future for the Church that **no one** is expecting?

- Does "Darius the Mede" have a secret identity?

- Is there a relationship between Daniel's night in the lion's den and Cyrus's decree to rebuild Jerusalem?

- How can we learn to pray like Daniel?

- Did the 70 Weeks countdown inspire both the pilgrimage of the Magi and the Jewish Revolt of AD 70?

- Are there statements of Jesus in the Gospels that explain many of the truths hidden within this prophecy?

- Does the prophecy identify the region of the world from which the Antichrist will come?

- Does the organization of the "weeks" give us a clue as to the timing of the Rapture of the Church?

From this sampling of questions, I'm certain you can see that Daniel's *70 Weeks Prophecy* touches on a myriad of topics and is everything that the esteemed scholars at the beginning of the chapter said it would be. It is, indeed, the most important prophecy in the Bible.

For that reason, I consider this my most important book. It examines the panorama of eschatological topics, and it interprets them in radically new and *biblically* exciting ways. Hopefully, your walk with Jesus will be changed by reading it. That is my goal

In **Part Two: Daniel's Prayer**, we will begin our journey and examine the context for the prophecy. Hang on for an exciting ride!

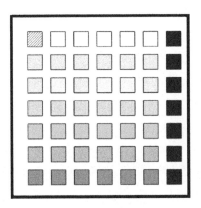

PART TWO:

DANIEL'S PRAYER

Chapter Two

DANIEL, DARIUS, AND THE PROPHETS

Daniel, observed in the books the number of the years which was revealed as the word of the Lord to Jeremiah the prophet for the completion of the desolations of Jerusalem, namely, seventy years. (Dan. 9:2)

The Book of Daniel, which is the source of the *70 Weeks Prophecy*, has also been the source of several popular books in Christian culture that have nothing to do with prophecy. They range from the practical diet book, *"The Daniel Plan,"* by Rick Warren and others to Anne Graham Lott's book, *"The Daniel Prayer,"* which is about the prayer in Dan. 9 that was answered by means of the *70 Weeks Prophecy.* Her book's comment about this prayer sums up my feelings about Daniel's prayer life:

> It is prayer that storms the gates of Heaven until things change. It is passionate, heartfelt, I-won't-let-You-go-until-You-bless-me pleading until you get an answer. It's the Daniel Prayer. — Anne Graham Lotz

Anne is the daughter of the late Billy Graham. She was born in 1948, the same year as the nation of Israel. She brilliantly captured the spirit of Daniel as he recorded his prayer and its answer. I recommend reading her book — and praying like Daniel!

11

THE SETTING

This prophecy and the prayer that precedes it are set in the first year of a king named Darius. Daniel precisely records the king's name, his lineage, and the year in which the prophecy was written:

> *In the first year of Darius, the son of Ahasuerus, of Median descent, who was made king over the kingdom of the Chaldeans — in the first year of his reign.* (Dan. 9:1-2 NASB)

Daniel also refers to this king in Dan. 6. He is the same king that famously was fooled into sentencing Daniel to the lion's den. Secular historians are quick to point out that no one named Darius ever reigned in Babylon. Atheists and Bible critics have jumped on this "obvious problem" to cast doubt on the entire Book of Daniel. Their theory is that Daniel was a forgery written hundreds of years later. They believe this forger or pseudo-Daniel confused the later Persian King, Darius the Great, with Cyrus who was the king who invaded Babylon, combining them into the king "Darius the Mede."

Their critique is a good example of why we have not completely solved the mystery of the *70 Weeks Prophecy*. **We trust secular historians** — 2500 years removed from events — over an eye-witness like Daniel.

Christians often trust secular historians rather than the inspired Word of God.

This is an incredibly important point, not just in regard to this chapter, but in regard to the entire book. We must not trust only our traditions, they are often mistaken. We need to dig deeply for the truth. Later in this chapter we will present new evidence that completely blows the atheists' arguments out of the water. But first let's look at the critics' claims logically.

The Book of Daniel and the included *70 Weeks Prophecy* are widely accepted by both the Jewish and Christian community. Daniel is part of the canon of Scripture of both faiths. Jesus refers to the Book of Daniel dozens and dozens of times; and He took for himself the title, the *Son of Man*, which comes from Dan. 7:13-14. If Daniel is not an inspired book and was written by a forger, Jesus is not the infallible Son of God. It's as simple as that since Jesus mentioned Daniel by name, called him a prophet (in Matt. 24:15), and based a significant portion of his teaching on the Book of Daniel.

As we will also learn later in this chapter, the Jews were carefully counting the years since their return from Babylon, based on the *70 Weeks Prophecy*. For reference, they also had the rest of the Prophets and Chronicles, which discuss the chronology of Persian Kings. It is **impossible** to believe a forger could have fooled the Jewish leaders with a book with an obvious error in its chronology. There must be another explanation.

I think we can be certain that this Darius ruled in Babylon at the time that Daniel indicated. And his true identity is revealed when we compare the Septuagint (LXX) and Masoretic Hebrew text (NASB translation) of Dan. 11:1:

*And I, in the first year of **Cyrus,** stood to strengthen and confirm him.* (Dan. 11:1 LXX, emphasis mine)

*In the first year of **Darius the Mede**, I arose to be an encouragement and a protection for him.* (Dan. 11:1 NASB, emphasis mine)

This parallel between the two texts shows that Darius the Mede was another name for Cyrus the Great. The reason that Cyrus went by another name is that "Darius" is a title or throne name, not an actual name.

The name Darius — or *Darayavahus* in Persian — is a nominative form, meaning "he who holds firm the good(ness)." Much as "Pharaoh" was a title of the Egyptian rulers and not a true name, the names of Persian kings found in our Scriptures (e.g. Darius, Ahasuerus, Artaxerxes, and Xerxes) may all have been titles, as well. If this is true, it adds incredible complexity to the chronology of Persian and Median kings, as many of them held one or more of these titles.

> **If the titles Darius, Ahasuerus, Artaxerxes, and Xerxes are not proper names, aspects of the currently-imagined biblical chronology of Persian Kings becomes questionable.**

This is another important point for you to remember as we explore the *70 Weeks Prophecy* in future chapters. For our purposes here, we need to strongly consider that the name "Darius" found in Dan. 6 and 9 was likely a "throne name" or a title, not the man's proper name.

Although the comparison of the LXX and NASB of Dan. 11:1 proves that Darius was Cyrus, we need to examine all other aspects of this theory to be completely convinced.

There are two primary theories about who this "Darius" was. One theory is that "Darius the Mede" was the General, Gobryas, who led the Persian forces when they conquered Babylon. The second theory is that he was Cyrus the Great himself as we have already seen.

Gobryas is thought by most to have died less than a month after the conquest of Babylon.[5] It is highly unlikely that the events of Dan. 6 and 9 could have taken place during that one-month period. However, William Shea, the biblical historian, has presented evidence that Gobryas may actually have survived an additional year, based on the *Chronicle of Nabonidus*, in which his death is recorded. Shea also presented evidence that economic documents referencing Cyrus do not refer to him as King of Babylon until one year after the conquest.[6]

Shea combined these two pieces of evidence to conclude that Cyrus could have appointed his General, Gobryas, as a vassal king until Gobryas died a year later. According to Shea's theory, Cyrus then would have assumed the combined throne of Babylon and Persia. In this way, Shea proposed that Gobryas was the mysterious Darius the Mede.

---

[5]"Chronicle of Nabonidus," last updated unknown, accessed Feb. 3, 2018, http://prophetess.lstc.edu/~rklein/Documents/chronnab.htm
[6] "Darius the Mede: An Update," *Andrews University Seminary Studies*, Autumn 1982, Vol. 20, No. 3, 229-247.

In order to determine whether Cyrus or Gobryas was Darius the Mede, we need to examine the four evidences found in Daniel's account. **However, whichever character it was, it is obvious that the name "Darius" was *not* his proper name and was instead a throne name**.

Dan. 9:1-2 and Dan. 5:30- 6:1 give us the four clues to his identity:

- He was the son of Ahasuerus, most likely a King of the Medes
- He was of Median descent.
- He was 62 years old when he ascended the throne
- He appointed 120 satraps (governors).

DARIUS THE MEDE

The first two facts are that "Darius" was a Mede and that he was the son of Ahasuerus. Now as we've indicated, "Darius" was a throne name and title, and "Ahasuerus" was most likely one, as well. The name "Ahasuerus" is "Xerxes" in Persian, meaning "hero among rulers." Cyrus was the son of the Persian Cambyses I (who could possibly have been titled Xerxes) and grandson of Astyages, who was a Median king (who also could possibly have been titled Xerxes).[7] In this way, Cyrus was of both Persian and Median royal descent. At one point, he defeated his grandfather, Astyages, to become king of both the Persians and Medes. In fact, the Medes revolted against his grandfather and handed him over to Cyrus prior to the battle. Even though he was a conqueror, he was readily accepted by the Medes

---

[7] "Life and Legend of Cyrus II," *World History*, last updated unknown, accessed Feb. 3, 2018, http://history-world.org/cyrusIII.htm

because he was "one of them." So he was of Median royal descent, just as Daniel states when he refers to Darius the Mede.

Gobryas is a minor character in secular history, and as such, little is known about his lineage. Xenophon, the historian, referred to him as an Assyrian, however, Xenophon was known to be inaccurate in many aspects of his account.[8] But whether Xenophon was correct or inaccurate, there is no evidence that Gobryas was a Mede or the son of a king.

In these first two of the four evidences for Darius's identity, Cyrus is consistent and Gobryas is not, just as we would expect. But the question must be asked: Why would Daniel make such an issue of claiming Darius was a Mede and not a Persian? Today, we generally focus on Cyrus's Persian ancestry. As we will discover in the next section, Daniel was a student of the prophets. As such, he was likely aware that Isaiah had prophesied in multiple places that Babylon would be conquered by the Medes (and Persians).

*Behold, I am going to stir up the **Medes** against them, who will not value silver or take pleasure in gold . . . And Babylon, the beauty of kingdoms, the glory of the Chaldeans' pride, will be as when God overthrew Sodom and Gomorrah.* (Isa. 13, 17,19 NASB, emphasis mine)

*Go up, Elam (Persia), lay siege, **Media**; I have made an end of all the groaning she has caused . . . And one said, "Fallen, fallen is*

---

[8] "Darius the Mede: An Update," 247

Babylon; and all the images of her gods are shattered on the ground."

(Isa. 21:2,9 NASB, clarification and emphasis mine)

So in Dan. 6 and 9, when the conqueror of Babylon is mentioned, the Holy Spirit stressed his Median ancestry to Daniel.

These two facts then — that Cyrus was a Mede and that he was the son of a king — are entirely consistent with Cyrus and probably very few, if any, other Persians who invaded Babylon — including Gobryas.

Historians also believe that Cyrus was most likely 62 years old when he ascended to the throne of Babylon, just as was indicated by Daniel, although his actual year of birth is shrouded in history.

Daniel informs us that Darius the Mede appointed 120 governors. The *Chronicle of Nabonidus* does indicate that Gobryas appointed sub-governors in Babylon. However, this was likely within the *city* of Babylon only and not for the entire nation, as the *Chronicle* primarily makes references to cities not nations. The appointment of such a large number of officials (120) would probably also not have been left to an interim leader like Gobryas. It was a task that only Cyrus himself would likely have undertaken. Finally, this *Chronicle* refers to Gobryas as only the Governor, not a king.

William Shea, the greatest critic of the "Cyrus as Darius" equivalency, acknowledges that Cyrus is a good match with the four facts about Darius as presented by Daniel. However, he asks one additional question: "Why does Daniel refer to both the third year of Cyrus (Dan. 10:1) and the first year of Darius the Mede (Dan. 11:1) in the same vision (Daniel's *Great Vision Prophecy* in Dan. 10-12)?" This question about why

Daniel would use TWO names for one king seems to contradict Cyrus being Darius the Mede.[9] And this use of BOTH names in Daniel is the main reason that Gobryas is the primary candidate for Darius the Mede in the minds of many churchgoers today.

This use of two names is actually quite easy to explain. The first use referenced by Shea in Dan. 10:1 is likely the writing of a scribe who collated the Book of Daniel, not Daniel's actual words. Daniel would have never referred to himself in the third person:

> *In the third year of* **Cyrus** *king of Persia, a message was revealed to Daniel, who was named Belteshazzar.* (Dan. 10:1 NASB)

In the Book of Daniel, the prophet himself never uses the name "Cyrus." Daniel's references to this king in Dan. 5:31, 6:1, 6:6, 6:9, 6:25, 6:28, 9:1, and 11:1 always use the names "Darius" or "Darius the Mede." There is one other reference to the name "Cyrus" in the Masoretic text of the Book of Daniel; not surprisingly, it is also the writing of the scribe, again referring to Daniel in the third person:

> *So this Daniel enjoyed success in the reign of Darius* **and in** *the reign of Cyrus the Persian.* (Dan. 6:28 NASB, emphasis mine)

If we closely examine this verse, it seems to preclude Darius and Cyrus from being the same person. It seems to refer to two kings. However, it is possible that the Hebrew passage in the NASB may actually say something

---

[9] "Darius the Mede: An Update," 232-233.

quite different than what we see translated. This theory was first proposed by D. J. Wiseman.[10]

> The basis of the hypothesis is that Daniel 6:28 can be translated 'Daniel prospered in the reign of Darius, *even (namely, or i.e.)* the reign of Cyrus the Persian.' Such a use of the appositional or explicative Hebrew "waw" construction has long been recognized in Chronicles 5:26 (*'So the God of Israel stirred up the spirit of Pul king of Assyria even the spirit of Tiglath–pileser king of Assyria'*) and elsewhere. — D. J. Wiseman

Wiseman's point centers around the Hebrew word "waw" (‫ו‬). This word can function as a simple conjunction ("and") or in a host of other ways. "Waw" is much more expressive and is utilized in a greater variety of ways than the English "and." One of these ways is to equate two items. This use is known as a "*hendiadys.*" That is the use found in 1 Chron. 5:26 about the Assyrian King Tiglath-pileser whose throne title was "Pul" or "Pulu." The construction in Dan. 6:28 is identical to 1 Chron. 5:26. The NIV, NLT, HCSB, and TNIV all provide footnotes that Wiseman's translation of Dan. 6:28 is an acceptable alternative to the NASB translation.

This hendiadys fits perfectly with our proposed reasons for the uses of the names "Cyrus" and "Darius" in the Book of Daniel. In the court of

---

[10] D. J. Wiseman, "Some Historical Problems in the Book of Daniel," D. J. Wiseman, ed., Notes on Some Problems in the Book of Daniel. London: The Tyndale Press, 1965. pp. 9-18.

Babylon during the days of Daniel, Cyrus was likely referred to by the throne name "Darius." That may be why Daniel only refers to him by this name. If the Book of Daniel was collated by a scribe years later when the name "Cyrus" was in common use, the scribe may have desired to clarify this possible misconception. The scribe likely entered the hendiadys in Dan. 6:28 to explain to his readers in no uncertain terms that **Darius the Mede** *was* **Cyrus.** This is completely consistent with the comparison between the LXX and the Masoretic (Hebrew) text of Dan. 11:1 that we examined at the beginning of the chapter.

This brand-new understanding of the historic uses of "Cyrus" and "Darius" in the Masoretic Hebrew text finally and conclusively solves the mystery of "Darius the Mede," which has puzzled the Church for hundreds of years.

It is historically interesting and mildly important in the context of this chapter. In subsequent chapters, it will be even more crucial to our understanding of how the Bible's chronology fits with our knowledge of the secular Persian Kings.

It is also of importance in discounting the atheist arguments that Daniel was a forgery. First, it provides the true identity of Darius the Mede, which ends their argument. But of equal importance, notice the ancient scribe's careful maintenance of Daniel's actual words. A simple solution for the scribe would have been to substitute the name "Cyrus" for "Darius the Mede" in Daniel's writings. But the scribe didn't do that; instead, he inserted an explanatory comment in Dan. 6:28 and preserved Daniel's inspired words, *despite* fully understanding that this was confusing given his culture's use of the name "Cyrus" instead of "Darius."

Of all the evidence I've ever seen of why Daniel is not a forgery, this is the strongest. No forger would ever insert an explanatory comment into his forgery. Only a scribe who desired to preserve the divine nature of that original document would have written the manuscript this way.

Who was this scribe who collated Daniel? We may never know, but my intuition tells me it was the same chronicler who also wrote Chronicles and the Books of Ezra and Nehemiah.

DANIEL AND THE PROPHETS

By establishing that Darius the Mede was a title for Cyrus the Great, we have confirmed the date on which Daniel prayed his great prayer in Dan. 9 — **the first year of Cyrus's reign** in Babylon. Historians tell us that Cyrus entered the city of Babylon on Oct. 29, 539 BC; it can therefore be assumed that the first year of his reign was the following year, 538 BC. This was 67 years after Daniel had been taken captive by Nebuchadnezzar, in 605 BC.

The sudden defeat of Babylon — the nation that had taken Daniel captive and destroyed Jerusalem — certainly must have caught his attention. We can be sure that he also noticed that its conqueror was a Mede, just as prophesied by Isaiah. I am also certain that at this point, Daniel began to wonder what lay in store for him, his nation, and his Temple. Would it be rebuilt? Daniel studied the writings of Jeremiah the prophet and saw the fate of Babylon prophesied:

"This whole land will be a desolation and a horror, and these nations will serve the king of Babylon seventy years. Then it will be **when seventy years are completed I will punish the king of Babylon** *and that nation," declares the Lord, "for their iniquity, and the land of the Chaldeans; and I will make it an everlasting desolation."* (Jer. 25:11-12 NASB, emphasis mine)

I am equally certain that when Daniel read in a later passage that the desolation of Jerusalem was only to last 70 years, he did the math; only three years remained before Jerusalem's desolation was to end!

For thus says the Lord, **'When seventy years have been completed** *for Babylon, I will visit you and fulfill My good word to you,* **to bring you back to this place.** (Jer. 29:10 NASB)

Daniel also undoubtedly read about the cause of his nation's exile and servitude to Babylon:

Therefore thus says the Lord of hosts, **"Because you have not obeyed my words,** *behold, I will send and take all the families of the north," declares the Lord, "and I will send to Nebuchadnezzar king of Babylon, My servant, and will bring them against this land and against its inhabitants and against all these nations round about; and I will utterly destroy them and make them a horror and a hissing, and an everlasting desolation."* (Jer. 25:8-9 NASB, emphasis mine)

The statement, *"Because you have not obeyed my words,"* may have weighed heavily on Daniel. So he set about to set things right before the Lord and prayed this great prayer of repentance we find in Daniel 9.

Drawing by Gustave Dore

DANIEL AND THE LIONS

Nearly every Sunday school student above the age of six is familiar with the account of Daniel in the lion's den. From this account, they have learned how Darius the Mede was tricked into creating a law which he could not reverse. This law made it illegal for anyone to pray to any god but the king for an entire month. We know from Scripture that Daniel faithfully continued to pray to the one true God, YHWH, despite this law. We also know that because of his faith, he spent a night with hungry lions.

However, what few have considered is that Daniel's prayer in Dan. 9 may have been *the* prayer that caused his arrest. Both his prayer and the lion's den event most likely took place in the first year of Darius. Even if we do not know the exact time of this prayer, we can be certain that the lion's den event happened at a time in near proximity to this wonderful prayer. And the Dan. 9 prayer may have influenced the outcome of the lion's den event, as we will see.

After Daniel survived the night with the lions, Darius (Cyrus) was so moved, so amazed by the power of YHWH, that he made this proclamation:

> *Then Darius the king wrote to all the peoples, nations and men of every language who were living in all the land: "May your peace abound! I make a decree that in all the dominion of my kingdom men are to fear and tremble before the God of Daniel; for He is the living God and enduring forever, and His kingdom is one which will not be destroyed, and His dominion will be forever."* (Dan. 6:25-26 NASB)

Wow! Is it any wonder that this same Darius (Cyrus) might then declare another proclamation **allowing the Jews to return to Jerusalem** and rebuild the Temple? Where did Cyrus get this idea to allow the Jews to return? Could it have come from Daniel himself? Might the night with the lions have prompted Cyrus to ask Daniel, "What can I do to honor your God?" Daniel may have found his answer as he contemplated the context of the *70 Weeks Prophecy*. I can almost hear Daniel asking the king, "Please, allow my people to return to Jerusalem."

OUR APPLICATION OF DANIEL'S LION DEN EXPERIENCE

There are spiritual principles and a pattern in this account that we should consider and apply in our own lives:

- World events may line up with prophecy; in Daniel's life, the event was the fall of Babylon.

- These events should drive us to the Word of God, just as it did Daniel.

- Study of God's Word may reveal the next event that God has ordained. In Daniel's life, this was the end of Jerusalem's desolation.

- This study of God's Word should cause us to fall on our knees in prayer.

- Our adversary, Satan, knows that prayer is the most powerful weapon on earth and will likely oppose us. In Daniel's life, this opposition was a night in the lion's den.

- Our faith *through* trial and opposition may inspire others throughout the world to embrace new realities in God.

- Through each step of the pattern, God will be glorified.

Understanding that Daniel may have been given knowledge of the *70 Weeks Prophecy* at or about the time of his trial in the lion's den is an exciting possibility. The possible links between this trial and the eventual answer to his prayer (the return to Jerusalem) is even more exciting. Might God use our lives in similar ways if we just seek him in prayer as Daniel did?

In the later chapters of this book, we discuss the strong possibility that God has planned amazing things, Spirit-enabled things, for the Church to accomplish before his return. When you read those portions of the book that concern the "heroic future" of the Church, consider praying a "Daniel Prayer," asking God to bring that reality about.

In the next chapter, we'll begin to examine the original prayer that initiated the rest of biblical history!

Chapter Three

DANIEL'S PRAYER OF REPENTANCE

So I gave my attention to the Lord God to seek Him by prayer and supplications, with fasting, sackcloth and ashes. I prayed to the Lord my God and confessed. (Dan. 9:3-4 NASB)

In Chapter Two, we discovered that Daniel's study of God's Word led him to understand that the return of his people to Jerusalem was at hand. We also discovered that Daniel understood the severity of the sin that had caused God to punish his nation. Therefore, Daniel, in humility and fasting, came before the Lord on behalf of his people.

Have you ever repented for the sins of your nation or your church? Westerners are notoriously self-focused. We view our sin as individual and our repentance as personal. Daniel, however, did not. Although Ezekiel referred to him as a man of outstanding personal righteousness (Ezek. 14:14), Daniel knew that he had been judged along with all of Israel during the 70-year captivity. And he repented in a very Hebraic, corporate way. I think there is a lot to learn from Daniel's approach.

He also began his prayer in a most unusual way — by reminding God of his covenant and promises.

*Alas, O Lord, the great and awesome God, who keeps his **covenant and lovingkindness** for those who love Him and keep His commandments. (Dan. 9:4 NASB, emphasis mine)*

Anyone who studies the *70 Weeks Prophecy* should have this verse highlighted, in my opinion. The rest of this chapter — including the rest of Daniel's prayer and the angel Gabriel's answer to Daniel — revolve around this initial verse. It's all about God's covenant and the lovingkindness of God. Daniel knew God was faithful, despite his nation's sin; and he appealed to that faithfulness. God keeps His promises.

So what covenant is Daniel referring to? It is highly instructive. I dare say that if you don't know, then you can't fully understand the *70 Weeks*. Let's find out what it all means.

THE DANIEL 9:4 COVENANT

The Old Testament contains four covenants and foretells a fifth. We will consider four of the five in our discussion of the *70 Weeks Prophecy* (we will ignore the Noahic Covenant):

- The Abrahamic Covenant (made with Abraham)
- The Mosaic Covenant (made with Israel and given to Moses)
- The Davidic Covenant (made with David)
- The New Covenant (to be ratified by the blood of Jesus)

Obviously, at the time of Daniel; the **New Covenant** had not yet been implemented, so he was not referring to this Covenant. Let's examine the other three Covenants to see which one Daniel was suggesting.

Davidic Covenant

God's covenant with David promised to establish David's throne forever. This promise was first made in II Sam. 7. Isaiah articulates it very well in the following passage:

> *Of the increase of his government and of peace there will be no end, on the **throne of David** and over his kingdom, to establish it and to uphold it with justice and with righteousness from this time forth and forevermore. The zeal of the Lord of hosts will do this.*
>
> (Isa. 9:7 NASB, emphasis mine)

There are several reasons why the covenant referred to in Dan. 9:4 isn't the Davidic Covenant. First, the Davidic covenant spoke only to the question of whose descendant would rule the nation and not to the restoration of the land, which was the primary purpose of Daniel's prayer.

Second, if Daniel was reading the scroll of Jeremiah, he would have been very aware of "Jeconiah's curse." We know from Scripture that Jeconiah was also known as Jehoiachin. Daniel would most likely have known Jeconiah personally, as he was King of Judah when Daniel was deported to Babylon. Jeremiah records the curse:

> *Thus says the Lord: "Write this man down as childless, a man who shall not succeed in his days, for none of his offspring shall succeed in sitting on the throne of David and ruling again in Judah."*
>
> (Jer. 22:30 NASB)

At first glance, this curse seems to invalidate the Davidic Covenant (Jeconiah was a descendant of David). Although we know that it did not, in Daniel's mind it may well have appeared that God was rescinding a promise He had made years earlier.

Let's take a brief moment to discuss how God overcame Jeconiah's curse, thereby allowing Jesus to become His eternal King on David's throne. As you may know, Joseph was a direct descendant of the Davidic kingly line. Jesus, however, was conceived by the Holy Spirit, and was therefore not born into Jeconiah's line. However, Jesus was *adopted* by Joseph; in this way, he *inherited* the right to rule on David's throne, thereby bypassing the curse placed on Joseph's physical descendants. Only the true God could have created an arrangement in which a miracle (conception by the Holy Spirit) would be the only means by which to fulfill His promise.

Mosaic Covenant

The second covenant was the Mosaic Covenant. It's primarily found in Deut. 11. It was a conditional Covenant, in that it promised either God's blessings for obedience or curses for disobedience, dependent entirely on the actions of His people:

> *See, I am setting before you today a blessing and a curse: the blessing,*
> *if you obey the commandments of the Lord your God, which I command*
> *you today, and the curse, if you do not obey the commandments of the*
> *Lord your God but turn aside from the way that I am commanding*
> *you today.* (Deut. 11:26-28 NASB)

Daniel was very aware of this second Covenant and refers to it directly in his prayer.

> *We have rebelled against him and have not obeyed the voice of the Lord our God by walking in his laws, which he* **set before us** *by his servants the prophets. All Israel has transgressed your law and turned aside, refusing to obey your voice. And the* **curse** *and oath that are written in the* **Law of Moses** *the servant of God have been poured out upon us, because we have sinned against him.* (Dan. 9:9-11 NASB, emphasis mine)

Daniel is directly quoting from Deut. 11 in this portion of the prayer. Notice how Daniel uses the phrases "*set before us*" and the "*the curse*" in referencing the promises made by God in the Mosaic Covenant.

In his prayer, Daniel clearly acknowledges the sin of Israel and the righteous act of God in punishing his wayward people. The Mosaic Covenant was fulfilled just as God had said it would be.

So Daniel's prayer was not a supplication for something he felt God owed His people. No, Daniel was appealing for grace. He was asking for what his people didn't deserve, trusting solely in the mercy of God.

We are left with just one covenant. Daniel must therefore have been referring to the Abrahamic Covenant in Dan. 9:4.

Abrahamic Covenant

God's promises to Abraham were numerous. Some were personal. God promised that He would make Abraham's name great (Gen. 12:2), that

Abraham would have numerous descendants (Gen. 13:16), and that he would be the father of many nations (Gen. 17:4-5).

God also promised two things to the future nation of Israel:

- They were promised the land of Israel. (Gen.12:7; 13:14-15; 15:18-21), and

- They were also promised that all the nations of the world would be blessed through the seed of Abraham (Genesis 12:3; 22:18). This was a reference to the Messiah.

It is primarily the first of these corporate, national promises that Daniel referred to in Dan. 9:4. If God had promised the nation of Israel that they would possess the land of Israel forever, then Daniel had *faith* that God would restore them to that land. God keeps His promises.

However, God had a surprise in store for Daniel, as well. Not only was God going to address the land aspects of the Abrahamic Covenant, He was also going to reveal the coming of the Messiah, the one who would be the blessing for all nations and who would eventually do away with Israel's sin forever.

What is truly amazing about the Abrahamic Covenant is that — unlike the Mosaic Covenant — it was a unilateral Covenant. In the bilateral Mosaic Covenant, Israel was punished for breaking the rules. In the Abrahamic Covenant, God himself paid the price if Israel broke its promises. How wonderful is our God!

Drawing by Gustave Dore

Cutting a Covenant

God "cut" the **Abrahamic Covenant** with Abraham and Israel. This word "cut" (Heb.: karath) is where we get the slang English term "cutting a deal." This phrase is based on an ancient Middle Eastern custom in which animals were cut in half, and the two parties of a covenant would walk between the pieces, saying in essence, "If I break this covenant, let this (the act of being cut in half) be done to me." When God "cut" the Covenant with Abraham, only he walked between the animal pieces:

> *It came about when the sun had set, that it was very dark, and behold, there appeared a smoking oven and a flaming torch which passed between these pieces. On that day the Lord made a covenant with Abram, saying, "To your descendants I have given this land."* (Gen. 15:17-18 NASB)

Since only God walked between the pieces, He was saying in essence, "Abraham if you or your descendants break this Covenant, let this be done to *Me*." This "too-good-to-be-true" provision is the unilateral aspect of the Covenant.

Later in the *70 Weeks Prophecy* the angel Gabriel would use this same Hebrew word, *karath,* in regard to the Messiah:

> *Then after the sixty-two weeks the Messiah will be cut off (karath) and have nothing.* (Dan. 9:26 NASB)

This Hebrew word, *karath,* means to "cut down", "cut," or "kill." Based on this translation, the vast majority of biblical scholars have considered this verse to refer to Jesus's crucifixion; and I agree. Isaiah gives a fuller rendering of this same Hebrew word:

He was cut off (karath) out of the land of the living for the transgression of my people. (Isa. 53:8 NASB)

This verse confirms that Dan. 9:26 is speaking about the crucifixion, after which Jesus was "cut off" from the land of the living (he was killed). Not only was He killed, but it was for the transgressions of Israel, Daniel's and Isaiah's people. Therefore, when Dan. 9:26 says that the Messiah was "cut off," it is a descriptive fulfillment of the Covenant made with Abraham. Jesus paid the price when Israel (and all of us by means of our sin) broke God's Covenants. We must never diminish Jesus's amazing love that he poured out for us on the cross. "*But God demonstrates his own love toward us, in that while we were yet sinners, Christ died for us*" (Rom. 5:8 NASB).

PRAYING FOR AN ANSWER

Daniel opened his prayer of repentance with an appeal to the Abrahamic Covenant. He ended it by directly stating that Israel did not deserve the mercy of God:

> *O my God, incline Your ear and hear! Open Your eyes and see our desolations and the city which is called by Your name; for we are not presenting our supplications before You on account of any merits of our own, but on account of Your great compassion. O Lord, hear! O Lord, forgive! O Lord, listen and take action!* (Dan. 9:18-19 NASB)

Although Daniel's primary goals in repenting the sins of his nation and calling upon God were the restoration of the land and the Temple, God's compassionate response addressed the underlying sin issue which caused the desolation of the land in the first place!

In the next Part of the book, **Part Three: 69 Weeks to the First Coming**, we'll begin to dissect and examine God's response to Daniel's prayer.

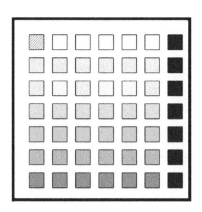

PART THREE

69 WEEKS TO THE FIRST COMING

Chapter Four

70 SHABUIM

Seventy **weeks** *have been decreed for your people and your holy city.*
(Dan. 9:24 NASB, emphasis mine)

Sometimes the answers to our prayers take months. Sometimes they take years. I began to pray for my Dad's salvation soon after I became a Christian in 1992. Fourteen years later, my Father placed his faith in Jesus and was saved.[11] Daniel didn't have to wait nearly as long for an answer to his prayer; Gabriel appeared while Daniel was still praying. The angel's words are instructive:

At the beginning of your supplications, the command was issued, and
I have come to tell you, for you are highly esteemed; so give heed to the
message and gain **understanding** *of the vision.*
(Dan. 9:23 NASB, emphasis mine)

From this verse we learn that God dispatched Gabriel to Daniel immediately. We also learn something truly important — Gabriel *expected* Daniel to **understand** the vision. In Chapter One, we discussed how this vision, the *70 Weeks Prophecy*, is difficult to fully understood today. Yet in

---

[11] The story of my father's salvation is an amazing work of God. It involved a dream, an interpretation of the dream, and an incredible sign. Read about it in Nelson Walters, *Revelation Deciphered*, (Ready for Jesus Publications, Wilmington, 2016), pp. 253-256.

this passage, the angel Gabriel expected Daniel to understand it 2500 years ago. What does this mean?

In my opinion, our lack of clarity about the vision today is primarily due to *tradition*. In other words, we have created speculative theories and taught them as truth. These abstract and probably false theories were all future to Daniel's time, so this wouldn't have clouded his understanding of the prophecy one bit. He had no preconceived notions or dates to worry about. This means that:

Daniel was able to understand the meaning of the vision and the mechanics that were used in calculating the time periods included in the vision.

Gabriel expected Daniel to understand the terms he used and the biblical passages he referenced. And he fully expected that Daniel would discern the meaning of this vision provided in response to Daniel's prayer. If Daniel could understand these things, we should be able to as well.

SHABUIM

When Gabriel made the following statement, he absolutely expected that Daniel would ***understand*** it:

> *Seventy **weeks** have been decreed for your people and your holy city.*
> (Dan. 9:24 NASB, emphasis mine)

In this context, "weeks" is an unusual phrase that is difficult to appreciate in our present culture. When we hear the term "weeks", we immediately think of a week of "seven days." The Hebrew word found in this passage is *shabuim*, which literally means "sevens." Although this could be a "seven" of anything, to Daniel the word would have conveyed a very specific Hebraic meaning, one that he would immediately have understood. It could be a week of seven days (Sunday – Saturday), or it could mean **a week of seven years**. After examining the length of the prophetic events that the fulfillment of these *shabuim* encompass, it is clear that the *shabuim* could not be a time period as short as days, but rather had to be years. Gabriel expected Daniel to understand the vision, and this was the **only meaning** of *shabuim* that Daniel would have understood.

ORGANIZATION OF THE SHABUIM

A Shabua (singular of Shabuim) is not just a "random" group of seven years. It is a very *specific* unit of time made up of seven *Hebraic* years. These years, in turn, are made up of months based on the cycles of the moon (alternating 29 or 30 days periods). Furthermore, the years are either twelve or thirteen months long, based on when the barley becomes ripe in Israel. In this way, the common (12-month) years are 353 to 355 days long (depending on lunar cycles), and the leap years (thirteen-months) are 383 to 385 days long. Over a nineteen-year period there are 235 lunar cycles, so the pattern of Hebraic common years and leap years repeat every nineteen years. In addition, this correspondence of solar and lunar cycles permits nineteen Hebraic years to equal nineteen 365-day years that we currently utilize in our secular culture's calendar.

By calculating Hebraic years in this way, they are in synch with both the solar cycles **and** lunar cycles. In Genesis, we learn that God designed these cycles for the establishment of years.

> *Then God said, "Let there be lights in the expanse of the heavens to separate the day from the night and let them be for signs and for* **seasons (Heb.: mod'edim)** *and for days and* **years.**"
> (Gen. 1:14 NASB, emphasis mine)

God also designed these cycles to indicate the timing of the *mo'edim* or God's appointed times (Feasts of the Lord). The *mo'edim* that occur in the Spring were exactly fulfilled by Jesus at his First Coming (on the exact day).[12] It has been postulated that the *mo'edim* that occur in the Autumn will be fulfilled by Jesus in similar manner at his Second Coming. Any "year" that does not exactly follow **both** the solar and lunar cycles, will cause the *mo'edim* to fall on incorrect dates.

The organization of a Shabua — seven Hebraic, solar/lunar years — is very specific. Our current culture typically accounts for time in a number system based on **ten**. To us, numbers like 10, 50, and 100 are even and logical number units. We call a group of ten years a decade. We group our music by decade: Music of the 60s, 70s, 80s, and 90s, etc. Our next larger division of years is the century, which is one hundred years. These divisions are normal and culturally natural to us.

---

[12] Joseph Lenard and Donald Zoller, *The Last Shofar!* (Xulon Press, 2014), pp. 97-129.

But, if we search for the Hebraic roots of our Christianity, we find that God gave ancient Israel a different numbering system. This system was based on the number **seven**, not ten. It was divided into six units of productive labor and one unit of rest—just as the week of seven days that we utilize today. God employed the same system to organize years for the people of Israel. Rather than use a decade of ten years, Israel used a *Shabua* of seven years. In the agricultural economy of Israel, this Shabua would mimic a week of days: For six years there would be productive toil; but for the final year, the sabbatical year — the **year of the Lord**, or "*Shmitah*" — the land would not be tilled or planted. It would lay fallow. A single Shabua of seven years graphically looks like this:

Figure 1: One Seven or Shabua

This division of years was God's commandment so that the land (and people) could rest and rejuvenate during the sabbatical year:

> *The Lord then spoke to Moses at Mount Sinai, saying, "Speak to the sons of Israel and say to them, 'When you come into the land which I shall give you, then the land shall have a sabbath to the Lord. Six years you shall sow your field, and six years you shall prune your vineyard and gather in its crop, but **during the seventh year the land shall have a sabbath rest**, a sabbath to the Lord; you shall*

not sow your field nor prune your vineyard.'" (Lev. 25:1–4 NASB, emphasis mine)

This organization of Hebraic years into a Shabua uniquely provides for both the proper timing of God's *mo'edim* and the sabbatical year during which the land was to lie fallow. Only a Shabua of seven Hebraic years can supply the appropriate timing of both of these features. For this reason, Shabuim "years" of alternative lengths (360 days or 14 months, etc.) are **not biblical**. Let me state that again, because it is critically important:

> **Only Shabuim consisting of seven Hebraic, solar/lunar years provide the correct timing of the *mo'edim* and sabbatical years. And only this type of Shabuim would have been understood by Daniel.**

In Chapter Six, we'll demonstrate how 69 of these biblical Shabuim provide a "precise" solution to the countdown of the *Seventy Weeks Prophecy*. However, because our Christian culture currently favors a solution to the countdown that features an "alternative length" Shabuim, there are some prophecy teachers who contest Daniel's use of "Shabuim" in Dan. 9:24. They will say, "But Lev. 25 doesn't use this *exact* word, *"shabuim."* It says "Sabbath" year and "seven years" rather than a *shabuim* of years; these aren't the same thing." That is a very poor argument because by referring to a "Sabbath," God was obviously showing Moses that a "week" (in which a Sabbath is an integral part) was in view. Additionally, in the Septuagint, the equivalent term "periods of seven," or *hebdomades,* is used in both Dan. 9:24 and Lev. 25: 1-4.

This concept of a "week" or Shabua of years is also older than Leviticus. In Genesis, when Jacob worked for Laban for the right to marry his daughters Leah and Rachel, Laban referred to a seven-year period as a "week."

> *Complete the* **week** *(Heb.* **shabua***) of this one, and we will give you the other (Rachel) also for the service which you shall serve with me for another* **seven years***.* (Gen. 29:27 NASB, clarification and emphasis mine)

There is no doubt that the reference in Dan. 9:24 is to weeks (*shabuim*) of years. That is what Daniel would *understand.*

GOD'S PERFECT SYMMETRY

More importantly, Daniel would understand that the 70-year exile was largely predicated on Israel's neglect of sabbatical years.

In II Chron. 36:21, we discover that the Babylonian exile was based on Israel *not* observing seventy sabbatical years (during a 490-year period) prior to the exile. God chose a punishment of 70 years so the land could rest for the seventy neglected sabbatical years. This punishment is a reference to a passage in Leviticus:

> *The land will enjoy its sabbaths all the days of the desolation, while you are in your enemies' land; then the land will rest and enjoy its*

sabbaths. All the days of its desolation it will observe the rest which it did not observe on your sabbaths, while you were living on it.

(Lev. 26:34-35 NASB)

We ultimately will discover that in the 70 Shabuim of the *70 Weeks Prophecy*, God would redeem Israel with seventy *additional* sabbatical years, creating a perfect symmetry. We illustrate the symmetry of the *70 Weeks Prophecy* in the following Figure:

Figure 2: Symmetry of Sabbatical Years

How could these 70 Shabuim be anything *but* sabbatical cycles of years? There were seventy sabbatical cycles of "sin" which led to seventy years of punishment. Gabriel told Daniel that God would then provide seventy more sabbatical cycles to bring about an end to sin. No wonder the *70 Weeks Prophecy* is regarded as *the most important prophecy* in the Bible!

Daniel would have understood Lev. 26:34-35 perfectly. Because he would have understood that the cause of the 70-year exile were 70 missed sabbatical cycles — as we have already seen — there is absolutely no doubt that he also would have understood the meaning of the additional 70 sabbatical years when these were suggested by Gabriel.

EXTRA-BIBLICAL SUPPORT

In addition to all the biblical evidence for the use of *Shabua* to refer to seven, Hebraic, solar/lunar years, there is extensive extra-biblical evidence. The word *Shabuim* or weeks is used in exactly this manner in the non-canonical Book of Jubilees. The Hebrew version of this book was unknown until the discovery of the *Dead Sea Scrolls.* Fifteen copies of this Hebrew manuscript (which included the word *Shabuim*) were found, and they clearly support our thesis here — that this word is a reference to a seven-year period.

The *Dead Sea Scrolls'* manuscipt, *the Damascus Document*, also directly references the *Shabuim* of the Book of Jubilees and confirms this word meant a sabbatical cycle of seven years as well.

> "And the exact statement of the epochs of Israel's blindness to all these, behold it can be learnt in the Book of the Divisions of Times (Book of Jubilees) into their Jubilees and **Weeks (Shabuim)**"

LARGER ORGANIZATION OF SHABUIM

Because this organization of time was a system based on seven instead of ten (no decades or centuries), God commanded Israel to organize years into seven sevens or seven shabuim (sabbatical) year groupings.

> *You are also to count off seven sabbaths of years for yourself,* **seven times seven years**, *so that you have the time of the seven sabbaths of years, namely, forty-nine years.* (Lev. 25:8 NASB)

This larger organization of years would graphically look like the Figure below:

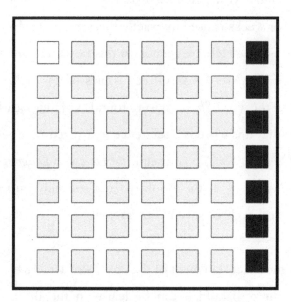

Figure 3: Seven Sevens or Shabuim

You may recognize that this graphic is similar to the one found at the beginning of each **Part** of this book. It is critically important to the understanding of the *70 Weeks Prophecy*.

These "seven sevens" or "seven sabbaths of years" are the building blocks of all longer periods of time in Hebraic thought. At the end of this period of seven sabbatical year cycles (49 years), God commanded Israel to observe a *Jubilee*, on the fiftieth year.

> *You are also to count off **seven sabbaths of years** for yourself,*
> ***seven times seven years**, so that you have the time of the seven*

sabbaths of years, namely, **forty-nine years**. *You shall then sound a ram's horn abroad on the tenth day of the seventh month; on the day of atonement you shall sound a horn all through your land. You shall thus consecrate* **the fiftieth year** *and proclaim a release through the land to all its inhabitants. It shall be a* **jubilee** *for you.* (Lev. 25:8–10 NASB, clarification and emphasis mine)

There are two ways to account for this fiftieth year, the *Jubilee* year. Traditional ten-based thinkers want to insert an extra year, the Jubilee year, between each grouping of forty-nine years. This rounds off the odd number based on sevens and creates a cycle of fifty years, a very modern concept. The following is a graphic of this method of accounting for a Jubilee. The striped block between the two forty-nine-year cycles represents the Jubilee year:

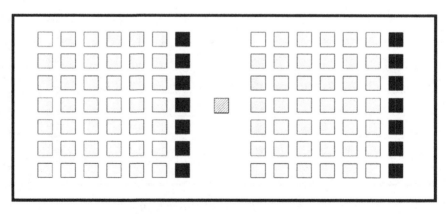

Figure 4: 50-Year Jubilee Cycle

Admittedly, we do not have an accurate historical reckoning of how the ancient Hebrews accounted for the Jubilee. But this seems an odd accounting of time to me (and others). Traditional weeks of days flow by in unbroken order. We don't, for instance, stop and insert a single-day holiday like Thanksgiving and then begin a new cycle of weeks. Rather, holidays are incorporated into the continuous flow of weeks that carry on for years, decades, and centuries.

A second view of how Israel might have accounted for Jubilees is that the first year of the next cycle became the Jubilee year. This second view makes more sense because it is both scripturally possible and allows for a continuous cycle of forty-nine-year groupings. I prefer this second view, as the Jubilee years do not interrupt the normal flow of years, allowing each seventh year to be a sabbatical year. This view is pictured below. Notice that the "striped" Jubilee years are also the first year of the *next cycle* in this arrangement:

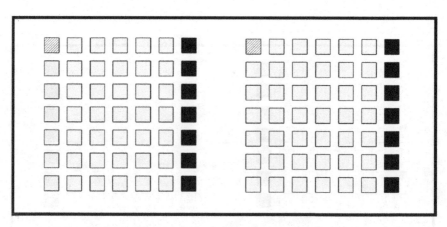

Figure 5: 49-Year Jubilee Cycle

The greatest support for a continual cycle of forty-nine years constituting a Jubilee cycle is found in the ancient Book of Jubilees, which we've already mentioned. Most likely written in the second century BC, the Book of Jubilees clearly utilizes a series of forty-nine years as a Jubilee cycle. And although the Book of Jubilees is not part of the canon of Scripture and therefore not inerrant, it was highly regarded during the time of Jesus and the early Church. It is referenced in the writings of Justin Martyr, Origen, and Eutychus; and it has been found among the Dead Sea Scrolls, as we've already seen. Certainly, a book about Jubilee cycles that was so highly regarded could not be in error about the *manner* by which the Jews accounted for Jubilees around the time of Jesus.

DANIEL'S SEVENTY WEEKS PROPHECY

Now that we have a grasp of the ancient Hebrew method of accounting for time, we are prepared to apply this concept to the *70 Weeks Prophecy*. As we've already seen, Gabriel told Daniel that 70 *Shabuim* were decreed. Daniel (and all Jews of his era) would have naturally assembled these years into forty-nine-year groupings (Figure 3). Viewed in this way, the prophecy is really about **ten Jubilee cycles** of forty-nine years each (490 years total).

The angel Gabriel's organization of the seventy Shabuim confirms that they truly are Jubilee cycles. He presented them to Daniel in three groupings, each representing different numbers of Jubilee cycles:

> *From the issuing of a decree to restore and rebuild Jerusalem until Messiah the Prince there will be seven weeks* [**one Jubilee cycle**] *and sixty-two weeks* [**eight complete Jubilee cycles and one incomplete Jubilee cycle**]. (Dan. 9:25 NASB, clarification and emphasis mine)

The prophecy also tells us of a unique last seventieth week, the 70th Week of Daniel:

> *And he will make a firm covenant with the many for* **one week** [shabua], *but in the middle of the* **week** [shabua] *he will put a stop to sacrifice and grain offering.* (Dan. 9:27 NASB, emphasis mine)

Daniel would have been able to easily imagine these shabuim as Jubilee cycles. A graphic of how he might have envisioned them follows:

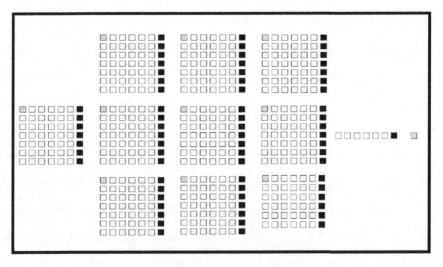

Figure 6: 70 Sevens or Shabuim

The single Jubilee cycle at the left of the graphic represents the initial seven weeks of Daniel's prophecy. The nine Jubilee cycles in the middle of the graphic are the sixty-two weeks. Notice, however, that the final Jubilee cycle is incomplete; the final Shabua (seven years) is missing. The missing Shabua is the single week at the far right of the graphic, which represents the *70th Week of Daniel*; and the final Jubilee year of this grouping is the striped square following the 70th Week.

I think this graphic is highly instructive. Today, we tend to think about the 70 weeks as 490 years or possibly 483 years plus a final period of seven years. We concern ourselves with how those years were prophesied and intersected with Jesus's ministry. As interesting as that might be (and we will examine this later in **Part Three**), the graphic serves best to depict how an ancient Israelite would look at the prophecy and the organization of sabbatical years and Jubilee years. Looking at the prophecy this way, it is immediately obvious that the final Jubilee cycle is incomplete and will not be fulfilled until the final *Shabua* (final seven-year period) occurs.

This *exact* model and interpretation is also found among the writings in the *Dead Sea Scrolls*. The following document, the *Melchizedek Peshser*, directly references the 70 Shabuim of Daniel 9:24-27 and confirms the representation of the **ten jubilee cycles**!

> "For He will restore them and proclaim freedom to them and make them abandon all of their sins. This shall take place during the sabbatical cycle (shabua) of the first jubilee following the nine jubilees, and on the Day of Atonement f[alling] at the **end of the jubilee, the tenth**." llQMelch 3 II, 4-8.

55

> This amazingly important find shows that Jews of the first and second centuries BC considered the *shabuim* of the Book of Daniel to be <u>sabbatical cycles with ten associated Jubilees</u>. It also clearly demonstrates that they considered that the Jubilee immediately following Daniel's 70th *Shabua* would usher in the Messianic age.

In future chapters, we will examine the implications of the final sabbatical year in the 70th *Shabua* of Daniel and the final Jubilee year. However, at this point, we simply need to understand that the *70 Weeks Prophecy* is essentially a vision about ten Jubilee cycles. This is the way Daniel would have **understood** it, and it's just as clear that this is the way the Jewish writers of the *Dead Sea Scrolls* **understood** it.

THE 70 SHABUIM AND FORGIVENESS

At this point, you may well be wondering why we have said that the final Jubilee cycle is incomplete. You might ask, "Wouldn't it make more sense if they were all continuous?" It would, but as we will discuss later, there are significant reasons to believe that the final Jubilee cycle *must* be interrupted, and that the final shabua *must* be in the future.

We will uncover a number of these reasons as we proceed throughout the book, but one reason is found in a most unlikely place and this is a good time to examine it. As we indicated in Chapter One, there are no references to the *Seventy Weeks Prophecy* in the Epistles or in Revelation. But there *is* a prominent one in the Gospels.

Then Peter came and said to Him, "Lord, how often shall my brother sin against me and I forgive him? Up to seven times?" Jesus said to him, "I do not say to you, up to seven times, but up to **seventy times seven.***"* (Matt. 18: 21-22 NASB, emphasis mine)

As you can see, this is the passage that inspired the title of this book, *70 Times 7*.

Peter asked Jesus a logical question, "*How often shall my brother sin against me and I forgive him?*" And he offered Jesus a suggestion, "*Up to seven times?*" Why did Peter choose this number? We don't know. But in Israel in that day, debts were forgiven during the final year or sabbatical year of a Shabua. Might Peter have been thinking along those terms? Was he thinking that sin debts would be forgiven in that year as well? We simply don't know. But — and this is very important — we do know Jesus *was* thinking of Shabuim when he answered Peter.

I do not say to you, up to seven times, but up to **seventy times seven.** (Matt. 18:22 NASB, emphasis mine)

Nearly every Bible scholar who has given their interpretation of this passage has assumed that Jesus simply meant "a very long time" or perhaps even "the rest of your life" when he used the phrase "seventy times seven." And while that interpretation is accurate, it misses the fact that this passage is a quote of the *70 Weeks Prophecy*. The **seventy "sevens" (Shabuim) are seventy times seven**! This phrase is an *exact* reference to Dan. 9:24.

Jesus then went on to explain this cryptic phrase—just in case his disciples weren't able to understand his reference—by telling the *Parable of the Unmerciful Servant*. In this familiar parable, the king (Jesus) forgives an enormous debt of 10,000 talents. (600,000 pounds of precious metal). Most bible scholars equate this huge obligation with our sin debt to God which Jesus paid when he was "cut off" (*karath*) on the cross.

This forgiveness of sins perfectly matches the purposes of the *70 Weeks Prophecy* which we will examine in the next chapter.

Immediately after being forgiven this enormous debt, however, the unmerciful servant refused to forgive even a small amount another servant owed him. In this way, Jesus elucidated to Peter and the other disciples how God views us when we are unwilling to forgive and demonstrated the hypocrisy of our unforgiveness.

70 TIMES SEVEN AND HISTORICISM

What nearly everyone has missed, however, is how this passage proves unequivocally that the prophecy is not yet completely fulfilled. Let's look at Jesus's statement one more time:

> *I do not say to you, up to seven times, but* **up to seventy times seven**. (Matt. 18:22 NASB, emphasis mine)

Jesus clarified for his disciples (and for us) that forgiveness is to be offered **up to and including** *seventy times seven* times. If this phrase truly refers to the 70 Shabuim of Daniel's prophecy, this means Christians are to forgive until the completion of all 70 Shabuim — **but not after**. Obviously, we are still living during a time where Jesus expects us to forgive. For this reason, it is just as obvious that the 70 Shabuim of the prophecy cannot have been completed yet — because we are still to forgive.

This has profound impact on prophecy. There are a significant number of biblical scholars (historicists and preterists) who believe the *70 Weeks Prophecy* was fulfilled in the first century. This section proves their theory is **categorically impossible**! This is so important, that it begs restating:

If forgiveness is to extend up to the completion of the 70 Shabuim but not after, the Shabuim cannot be completed yet because we are still commanded to forgive. The 70th Week of Daniel must extend into the future, <u>until the final return of Jesus</u>. This is absolute *proof* that the *70 Weeks Prophecy* has not yet been completely fulfilled.

We will support this conclusion with many other proofs throughout this book, but this evidence *alone* should be sufficient proof that the 70th or final Shabua of the 70 "Weeks" is a future event.

That is why the 70th Shabua of Daniel is pictured separately from the other Jubilee cycles. And that is also why this book has been given the title *70 Times 7.*

In the next chapter we will examine what God plans to accomplish during these 70 Shabuim.

Chapter Five

GOD'S GOALS FOR THE 70 WEEKS

"Seventy weeks have been decreed for your people and your holy city, to finish the transgression, to make an end of sin, to make atonement for iniquity, to bring in everlasting righteousness, to seal up vision and prophecy and to anoint the most holy place." (Dan. 9:24 NASB)

Very few biblical prophecies come with God's purposes clearly listed for us. The *70 Weeks Prophecy*, however, lists six purposes directly and implies three more — for a total of nine. Fulfilling these purposes will accomplish the Abrahamic Covenant, which was the topic of Daniel's prayer as we learned in Chapter Three. These nine purposes are:

1) To **rebuild Jerusalem** and the **Temple,**

2) To provide **a timetable to the First Coming of Messiah,**

3) To provide **a timetable to the Second Coming of Messiah,**

4) To **finish the transgression,**

5) To make **an end of sin,**

6) To **make atonement for iniquity,**

7) To **seal up vision and prophecy,**

8) To bring in **everlasting righteousness,** and

9) To **anoint the most holy.**

As you can imagine, these are massive purposes that must have excited Daniel beyond anything he had ever dreamed.

Rebuild Jerusalem and the Temple

Although, Gabriel did not mention the rebuilding of Jerusalem and the Temple in the six stated purposes at the beginning of the prophecy, the city and Temple figure prominently in every verse of the prophecy. In fact, the future history of the Temple and city are the second most important factor in the prophecy, second only to the revealing of the Messiah. Daniel prayed:

> *Let Your face shine on Your desolate sanctuary. O my God, incline Your ear and hear! Open Your eyes and see our desolations and the city which is called by Your name.* (Dan. 9:17-18 NASB).

And God responded.

> *It will be built again, with plaza and moat, even in times of distress.* (Dan. 9:25 NASB)

God did not stop there, however. He revealed that 69 Shabuim later, the Temple and city would be destroyed yet again:

> *The people of the prince who is to come will destroy the city and the sanctuary. And its end will come with a flood.* (Dan. 9:26 NASB)

In the Septuagint translation of the Book of Daniel, we see a third Temple arise.

And one week shall establish the covenant with many: and in the midst of the week my sacrifice and drink-offering shall be taken away: and **on the Temple** *shall be the abomination of desolations; and at the end of time an end shall be put to the desolation.* (Dan. 9:27 LXX, emphasis mine)

Daniel was given a panoramic view of the future of the Temple. It would be built again, but in times of distress. Then, it would once again be destroyed. Finally, a third Temple would arise; but an abomination would cause it to be desolate. Then, at the "end of time," the desolations would end. In this way, Daniel was given the long-term vision that the Temple would eventually be glorious and freed from its distress.

Provide a Timetable to the First and Second Comings of Messiah

The *70 Weeks Prophecy* is a countdown! It's a countdown to the First and Second Comings of Jesus. There may be controversy about the exact starting and ending times of the prophecy, but there can be no doubt that Jesus, our Messiah, is its ultimate destination.

In the next chapter, we will begin to explore the mechanics of the prophecy.

The remaining six goals are all "Messianic" goals. All of them will be accomplished by Jesus. They are a result of his victory over sin and the grave.

Drawing of New Jerusalem by Gustave Dore

Bring in Everlasting Righteousness

Righteousness is "rightness" with God. This phrase, found in Dan. 9:24, is parallel to Isa. 45:17, which says that Israel will be saved with an *everlasting* salvation. Both passages use an interesting "plural intensive" form of the Hebrew word for *everlasting*. Another rendering of this phrase in Dan. 9:24 might be: "righteousness of 'everlastingness.'" It speaks of eternity.

Eternal righteousness will only occur at the Second Coming of Jesus. Upon the resurrection of the dead, Daniel and all the Old Testament saints, all the dead in Christ, and all the living believers will be transformed in the blink of an eye into "resurrection" bodies, incapable of sin. At that time, eternal rightness with God will finally be achieved.

"Seal Up" Transgression, Sin, and Vision and Prophecy

Gabriel informed Daniel that three things will be sealed up: Transgression, sin, and vision and prophecy. Although our English translations use other words for "seal up," such as "finish" and "make an end of," the underlying Hebrew verb in each case is the same: *chatham*, meaning to "seal up." And regardless of which English word is used, the same action is in view. These items will be sealed away forever. So "*finish*" is a fine, modern English translation for this ancient concept.

It is important to notice that the transgression that is finished is not just a group of generic transgressions. It is the historic rebellion against God that started in the Garden of Eden that will be ended by the 70 Shabuim. It is *the* transgression.

When will transgression, sin, and all vision and prophecy be finished? Only upon the final and triumphant Second Coming of Jesus. Just as we saw with the phrase "everlasting righteousness," we simply cannot claim that the listed purposes of the 70 Shabuim were accomplished in the first century at Jesus's First Coming. The only explanation for the finishing of these things is that they will be completed at Jesus's Second Coming.

In fact, Jesus directly made reference to the sealing of vision and prophecy in the Gospels.

But when you see Jerusalem surrounded by armies, then recognize that her desolation is near. Then those who are in Judea must flee to the mountains, and those who are in the midst of the city must leave, and those who are in the country must not enter the city; because these are days of vengeance, **so that all things which are written will be fulfilled.** (Luke 21:20-22 NASB, emphasis mine)

Jesus is clear that an invasion of Jerusalem will take place during "the days of vengeance (when) *all* things that were written will be fulfilled," when prophecies and visions are sealed up and finished. This obviously did not happen during the first century and is proof that Luke 21:20-22 is not a reference to AD 70 but to a future destruction of Jerusalem. Many Old Testament and New Testament prophecies still remain incomplete. All things were not fulfilled in AD 70.

Make Atonement for Iniquity

Atonement is literally "cover." Obviously, the sacrificial death of Jesus on the cross for the sins of the world, once for all, is in view.

All of us like sheep have gone astray, each of us has turned to his own way; but the LORD has caused the iniquity of us all to fall on Him. (Isa. 53:6 NASB)

But even in this aspect, there is a shadow of both the First and Second Coming.

*Therefore, through this, Jacob's iniquity will be forgiven; and this will be the full price of the pardoning **[atonement]** of his sin: when he (Jesus) makes all the altar stones like pulverized chalk stones; when Asherim and incense altars will not stand.* (Isa. 27:9 NASB, clarification and emphasis mine)

Isa. 27:9 and the rest of Isa. 27 have the Second Coming in view. It is only at that time that Israel's atonement will truly be *realized*.

Anoint the Most Holy

This aspect, anointing the Most Holy, also has implications for First and Second Coming. After Jesus ascended to heaven, he entered the Holy of Holies in the heavenly Temple. There, acting as High Priest, He anointed it with His own blood.

But when Christ appeared as a high priest of the good things to come, He entered through the greater and more perfect tabernacle, not made with hands, that is to say, not of this creation; and not through the blood of goats and calves, but through His own blood, (Heb. 9:11-12 NASB)

However, in the Millennium, Jesus will anoint the Holy of Holies on earth in the Temple He builds according to the plans found in Ezekiel 40-48.

WITHIN THE 70 WEEKS OR AT THE END OF THE 70 WEEKS?

What is the timetable for accomplishing the nine purposes of the prophecy?

As we stated previously, there is a movement within Christianity that wishes to declare that the *70 Weeks Prophecy* was completed in the first century, shortly after the death and resurrection of Jesus. **This simply isn't correct**. As we have just seen, a large number of the stated purposes of the 70 Weeks can only be fulfilled upon the Second Coming.

Additionally, there are those who claim that all of the purposes must be fulfilled *within* the 70 Weeks and not during a "gap" period. They say this in order to force some aspects of the prophecy *into* the 70th Shabua. **Again, this simply isn't correct**. A careful examination of Gabriel's words to Daniel show that God's goals will be accomplished by *means* of 70 Weeks, not strictly *during* them:

> *Seventy weeks have been decreed for your people and your holy city, to finish the transgression, to make an end of sin, to make atonement for iniquity, to bring in everlasting righteousness, to seal up vision and prophecy and to anoint the most holy place.* (Dan. 9:24 NASB)

In the next chapter, we will begin to examine the specific aspects of the first 69 shabuim that lead to the First Coming of Jesus.

Chapter Six

COUNTDOWN TO THE FIRST COMING

"So you are to know and discern that from the issuing of a decree to restore and rebuild Jerusalem until Messiah the Prince there will be seven weeks and sixty-two weeks; it will be built again, with plaza and moat, even in times of distress." (Dan. 9:25 NASB)

We are now ready to begin to analyze the "countdown" to the First Coming of our Messiah, Jesus. Every countdown has a starting point, an ending point, and the time that lies between these two points. Precision events like a space launch have made such countdowns popular: ". . . seven, six, five, four, three, two, one, liftoff."

In the great countdown to the First Coming in Dan. 9:25, the starting point is the decree to rebuild Jerusalem, the ending point is the coming of Messiah the Prince, and the "countdown" is 69 sabbatical cycles or Shabuim. Obviously, these events were as precise as a space flight liftoff in the mind of the angel Gabriel. But unfortunately, our modern understanding of it isn't.

The countdown in this verse is the greatest mystery in this prophecy. We hope to shed light on it in this chapter.

THE COUNTDOWN AND FIRST CENTURY JEWS

There is very significant biblical and extra-biblical evidence that the first century Jews considered the *70 Weeks Prophecy* to be a countdown as well.

The Roman historian Tacitus made these comments about the first century Jews:

> In most [of the Jews] there was a firm persuasion, that **in the ancient records of their priests was contained a prediction** of how at this **very time** the East was to grow powerful, and rulers, coming from Judaea, were to acquire [a] universal empire. - Tacitus[13]

Notice that Tacitus reported that **most** Jews believed in a prophecy that predicted a Jew would rule the world, and that it would happen at a specific time. His contemporary, Suetonius, reported that this belief had spread "all over the Orient (Middle East)."[14] Not only did the Jews believe in this prophecy, but Josephus tells us that it was *the* primary driving force in causing them to revolt against Rome — which led to the destruction of the Temple in AD 70.

> But now, what did **most** elevate them in undertaking this war was **an ambiguous oracle that was also found in their sacred writings,** how "about that time, one from their country should become governor of the habitable earth."
> - Josephus[15]

---

[13] Tacitus, Histories, 5.13.
[14] Suetonius, *The Lives of the Caesars*, "The Deified Vespasian," 4.5.
[15] Josephus, Jewish War, 6.5.4.

So not only did the first century Jews believe in the *70 Weeks Prophecy*, they believed in it enough to go to war with the most powerful nation on earth. That is faith — misguided faith — but faith all the same.

There is also biblical evidence that the first century Jews had probably calculated the 69 Shabuim and were watching for Messiah the Prince. In the Gospel of John, we see that prior to Jesus's baptism, the Jewish authorities came to John the Baptist inquiring about Messianic issues:

> *The Jews sent to him priests and Levites from Jerusalem to ask him, "Who are you?" And he confessed and did not deny, but confessed, "I am not the Christ." They asked him, "What then? Are you Elijah?" And he said, "I am not." "Are you the Prophet?" And he answered, "No."* (John 1:19-21 NASB)

Why were they inquiring if a wilderness preacher like John was the Messiah or even Elijah (who was to precede the Messiah)? Was it that they had been counting the 69 Shabuim and thought this might be **the year** that the Messiah was to arrive? I believe this to be the case.

In Luke's Gospel, we see that *all* the people were in a state of expectation at the time of John's ministry. Was this because John's ministry coincided with the end of the 69 Shabuim?

> *Now while the people were in a **state of expectation** and all were wondering in their hearts about John, as to **whether he was the Christ**.* (Luke 3:15 NASB, emphasis mine)

Jesus, himself, seemed to expect that the Jews would have recognized him, in part, because this was the **time** of their visitation.

> *They will level you to the ground and your children within you, and they will not leave in you one stone upon another, because you did not recognize* **the time of your visitation.** (Luke 19:44 NASB, emphasis mine)

Jesus clearly expected the Jews of his day to recognize the **time** of his First Coming. He didn't expect them to recognize him, per se, but the **time** of God's visitation. In fact, their subsequent punishment in AD 70 was predicated on their lack of recognition. How did he expect them to recognize the time of visitation? Possibly a major way was for them to have calculated the 69 Shabuim to Messiah. Just as Gabriel expected Daniel to understand the prophecy, Jesus expected the first century Jews to understand it as well.

They could only calculate this countdown if they **understood** the starting point, the ending point, and what the Shabuim consisted of. And a period of seven traditional, Hebraic years is *exactly* what they would understand and calculate as we saw in the Dead Sea Scroll documents.

If many first century Jews missed the obvious — that Jesus was the Messiah — why did they later go to war, a suicidal war, based on this prophecy? We have no indications that they were following a messianic leader at that time. No, it probably means that they realized they had reached **the latest possible date for fulfillment of the prophecy**. Perhaps they hoped their messiah would arise during the war — that the war would cause him to reveal himself.

Obviously, that revealing did not happen. But, this probability — that they likely felt AD 70 was the latest possible date for the prophecy — offers us an amazing clue to validate the theory we will present in this chapter. We will examine this and other historic proofs later.

CALCULATING THE COUNTDOWN

If Jesus expected the first century Jews to be able to understand and calculate the countdown, we should be able to as well. There are at least four different decrees that have been suggested as the starting point and three possible end points. And none of the proposed combination solutions match **all** the aspects of the *70 Weeks Prophecy* perfectly. This is significant, so let me say that again:

> **None of the proposed solutions for the countdown to the First Coming of Jesus match the prophecy perfectly. Each one of them is missing one or more important aspects of the prophecy.**

Although Jesus expects us to understand and calculate the solution, it isn't simple. The answer is obvious once you see it; but as I said, it isn't simple. Let's begin by analyzing the four proposed starting points.

THE STARTING POINT: THE DECREE TO REBUILD

Four separate decrees have been suggested as the starting point, as shown in the following graphic on the next page:

Decree	Source	Explanation	Year
2 Chron. 36:22-23, Ezra 1:1-2	Cyrus	Command to rebuild the City and Temple	First year of Cyrus
Ezra 6:6-11	Darius	Command to resume work on the Temple	Second year of Darius
Ezra 7:1-21	Artaxerxes	Complete the Temple and Wall	Seventh year of Artaxerxes
Neh. 2:1-8	Artaxerxes	Repairing of the Wall – Not actually a decree	Twentieth year of Artaxerxes

Figure 7: Decrees to Rebuild

Now as we indicated before, none of the proposed solutions to the countdown match the prophecy exactly. Specifically, each decree is missing one or more important aspects. I believe there is a reason for this.

If you examine the first three decrees (the fourth "so-called decree" in the 20th year of Artaxerxes is never referred to as a decree in Scripture), you'll find that each one contains an aspect of the prophecy that the other one lacks. In other words, additively the first three decrees contain *all* necessary aspects of the prophecy. Is it possible that Christians have been searching for 2000 years for which **one** of the decrees was the prophetic decree, when it was a combination of the first **three** all along? If so, how can that be?

Is it possible that God authorized all the events that would take place, and the combined decrees of the three human kings were the **means** by which God implemented this command? This link between the command of God and the human decrees is found in the following **incredibly important verse**:

> *And they finished building according to the* **command of the God** *of Israel and* **the decree of Cyrus, Darius,** *and* **Artaxerxes** *king of Persia.* (Ezra 6:14 NASB, emphasis mine)

In this one verse, we see that the building (of the Temple and Jerusalem) was authorized by the command of God and then implemented by the three decrees of gentile kings — just as we are suggesting.

In Dan. 9:25, we are told the starting point was the issuing or "going forth" of the command. The Hebrew word translated "going forth" is *motsa*, which literally means "a spring which continually gives water." Was the implementation of God's command that "continual spring" of all the aspects of the prophecy by means of the three human decrees? If so, it shouldn't be surprising to us that each of these three human decrees are clearly referenced in the Book of Ezra as being *triggered* by the hand of God (Ezra 1:1, Ezra 6:22, Ezra 7:27).

None of the three decrees of Cyrus, Darius, and Artaxerxes—in-and-of-themselves—fulfilled *all* aspects of the prophecy. In my opinion, that is why none of the proposed past solutions to the countdown have been satisfactory. It was never fundamentally about human decrees; it was always about God and his Word!

This theory that the "decree" is actually the command by God implemented by the decrees of three gentile kings is **original to this book**. As such, I imagine you may be slightly skeptical at this point. We will continue to show evidence to support it as we work through this chapter so you can become more comfortable with the idea.

THE ENDING POINT: THE FIRST COMING OF MESSIAH

The coming of Messiah the Prince is the most important aspect of the countdown. Let's examine the potential end points next. Three possible end points have been proposed:

- The **birth** of Jesus
- The beginning of Jesus's ministry, probably his **baptism**
- His **rejection by the Jewish leaders** prior to his death on the cross

I am sure that as you read these three potential end points you realize that Bible scholars don't agree on the exact date of any of the events. Scholars have suggested possible dates; but frankly, the actual dates are shrouded in the mists of history. The scope of dates proposed for these potential end points range from 7 BC at the earliest to as late as AD 33. That is a range of 39 years! We don't know which of the end points Gabriel meant by the phrase "to Messiah the Prince," and the precise years of those events are in question.

However, I'd like to present my best guess. Messiah means "anointed," so the anointing of Jesus at his baptism by John the Baptist makes the most sense to me as the ending of the 69th Week of the prophecy. We have already discussed how in John 1, the Jewish leaders approached John the Baptist because they thought that year, the year of Jesus's baptism, might be the end point of the countdown.

Jesus gave us a second clue that this specific year was the end point of the 69 Shabuim. His reading from the scroll of Isaiah in the synagogue in Nazareth during the first year of his ministry contains the clue:

> *The Spirit of the Lord is upon Me because He anointed Me to preach the gospel to the poor. He has sent Me to proclaim release to the captives, and recovery of sight to the blind, to set free those who are oppressed, to proclaim the* **favorable year of the Lord**. (Luke 4:18-19 NSAB, emphasis mine)

Jesus indicated that this first year of his ministry was a Year of the Lord or sabbatical year. As we learned in Chapter Four, the final year of the 69th Shabuim was to be a Year of the Lord. Isaiah's prophecy, which Jesus quotes, states this particular Year of the Lord will be "favorable." It was the year that Israel was to meet Messiah the Prince face-to-face; it was a favorable year indeed.

And if this was truly the final year of the first 69 Shabuim, it is likely that the Bible would have identified it for us. In Luke 3:1-2, we learn that John the Baptist (who baptized Jesus) began his ministry in the fifteenth year of Tiberius Caesar, which historians believe was most likely AD 27[16].

---

[16] "When did the Ministry of John the Baptist Begin?" CARM.org, last modified: unknown, accessed Feb. 8, 2018, https://carm.org/when-did-the-ministry-of-john-the-baptist-begin

This is the only year of Jesus's ministry that is clearly identified by associating it with the reign of a gentile king.

Any of the dates in the full range of possible dates (7 BC to AD 33) is conceivable, however, every clue seems to point to AD 27 being the end point of the 69 Shabuim. Historical records of sabbatical years also seem to indicate AD 27 was a sabbatical year just as Jesus indicated in Luke 4. Additionally, 3 BC is the best estimate for Jesus's birth.[17] This would make Jesus "about 30 years of age" in AD 27 at the start of his ministry (Luke 3:23). The best estimate for the year of Jesus's crucifixion and resurrection is AD 30.[18] This also fits with a three-year ministry starting in AD 27.

> The most likely end point of the *70 Weeks Prophecy* is the baptism of Jesus [AD 27].

THE YEARS BETWEEN THE STARTING AND ENDING POINTS

Gabriel provided Daniel with the exact number of years between the starting and ending points of the countdown to Messiah the Prince.

> *From the issuing of a decree to restore and rebuild Jerusalem until Messiah the Prince there will be* **seven weeks** *and* **sixty-two weeks**; *it will be built again, with plaza and moat, even in times of distress.* (Dan. 9:25 NASB, emphasis mine)

---

[17] Joseph Lenard, *Mysteries of Jesus's Life Revealed* (Wordzworth, London, 2018), pp. 7-91. This book comprehensively assembles and examines facts about the date and place of Jesus's birth, death, and resurrection.
[18] Lenard, pp. 191-200.

Gabriel informed Daniel that there would be seven Shabuim (49 years) and sixty-two Shabuim (434 years) between the *decree to rebuild* and Messiah the Prince. If these two periods are contiguous and additive, we have a total of 483 years divided into two sections. Figuring back from our ending point of **AD 27** results in an anticipated starting point of **457 BC**. The following table examines the proposed starting and ending points.

Decree	Source	Year	483 Years Later
Ezra 1:1-2	Cyrus	538 BC	55 BC
Ezra 6:6-11	Darius	520 BC	37 BC
Ezra 7:1-21	**Artaxerxes**	**457 BC**	**AD 27**
Neh. 2:1-8	Artaxerxes	445 BC	AD 39

Figure 8: Potential 70 Weeks Starting Points

Our working theory is that the command of God authorized the first three decrees of the gentile kings. If this theory is correct, the countdown to Messiah the Prince should begin after all necessary aspects of the prophecy are fulfilled, which would be after the third decree. And at first glance, we seem to have a winner. The third decree, that of Artaxerxes found in Ezra 7:1-21, seems to be an exact match—69 Shabuim from this decree, Jesus's ministry began with his baptism. Mathematically, it is **exactly** what we would expect from the perfect word of God. But, we need to carefully examine all aspects of the prophecy to confirm that this theory is correct.

KEY ASPECTS OF THE DECREE TO REBUILD JERUSALEM

Let's look at the prophecy again, and then examine these aspects.

> *From the issuing of* **a decree** *to* **restore and rebuild** *Jerusalem until Messiah the Prince there will be* **seven weeks** *and* **sixty-two weeks**; *it will be built again,* **with plaza and moat**, *even in* **times of distress**. (Dan. 9:25 NASB, emphasis mine)

From this verse we can determine that there are six primary aspects of the prophecy that must be fulfilled:

- It must meet the biblical definition of a **decree.**
- It must contain provisions to "**restore** and **rebuild.**"
- It must be **7 and 62 Shabuim** from the decree to Messiah the Prince (we have already demonstrated this in the previous section).
- A **Plaza** and **Moat** must be built.
- There must be a **reason for the division of 7 and 62 Shabuim**.
- And the building of Jerusalem must take place during **times of distress**.

THE DECREE TO REBUILD

We have theorized that the command of God authorized the decrees of the gentile kings. This concept is completely consistent with Scripture. The word translated "decree" or "command" in Dan. 9:25 is the Hebrew word *dabar* meaning "word" not "decree." This is the same Hebrew term as found in the prophets, as in "the Word (*dabar*) of the Lord came to me." In the Septuagint, the equivalent Greek word in Dan. 9:25 is *logos* which also means "word."

God's command to rebuild certainly seems a better fit with *dabar* or *logos* than the decree of an earthly king.[19] And in Dan. 9:23, God gave a command (*dabar*). At the beginning of the angel Gabriel's answer to Daniel's prayer, he makes this statement:

> *At the beginning of your supplications, the command (**dabar**) was **issued**, and I have come to tell you, for you are highly esteemed.* (Dan. 9:23 NASB, emphasis mine)

What was this *dabar* or command? Was it simply God's command for Gabriel to come and give Daniel the prophecy? Or was it *the* command to rebuild Jerusalem and the Temple issued from the heavenly throne? The Hebrew word *dabar* is utilized in both Dan. 9:23 and 9:25, and there is great parallelism between them. Each *dabar* was "issued." The Hebrew construction is almost identical in the two verses.

If we re-read Dan. 9:23 again with fresh eyes, we can see the very strong likelihood that the *dabar* wasn't just *a* command for Gabriel to give Daniel the prophecy, but rather it was *the* command to answer Daniel's prayer — God had issued the command to rebuild the Temple. Gabriel said, "*The dabar* (to rebuild) *was issued and I have come to tell you!*" Gabriel was dispatched to let Daniel know that the command had already been given; and **Gabriel was excited** about it!

This first aspect is completely consistent with our working theory.

---

[19] William Struse, *Daniel's 70 Weeks*, (PalmoniQuest LCC, 2015), location 935-989. William Struse has done the Church a great service by pointing out that the command to rebuild is a "word" not a decree.

RESTORE AND REBUILD

It is also essential that we understand the exact meaning of the words the angel Gabriel used to describe the decree. In the NASB the Hebrew words in Dan. 9:25 are translated as *"restore"* and *"rebuild."* Let's examine them more closely. The second Hebrew word, *banah*, means "to build" and the equivalent word in the Greek Septuagint, *oikodomeó*, also means "to build a house." These terms are easy to understand and imply the rebuilding of Jerusalem.

But the first Hebrew word, *shûb*, is more difficult to understand. It's translated *"restore,"* and it appears over 1000 times in the Old Testament. Its primary definition is "to return" but in Dan. 9:25, the object of the verb is a city (Jerusalem). How does one "return" a city? In order to understand this usage, we must find a similar application.

In 2 Ki. 14 we learn that the city of Elath had been in ruins. Azariah, King of Judah, *"rebuilt [banah] Elath and restored [shûb] it to Judah"* (2 Ki. 14:22). These are the two *identical* verbs we found in Dan 9:25 — "to rebuild," and "to restore." In this context, the verb "to restore" means to allow it to function again under Israelite laws and rules (1 Kgs 12:21). *Rebuild* connotes a physical rebuilding of the walls and structures. *Restore* connotes a political and legal restoration.

As part of the first decree of Cyrus (in the first year of his reign), the Jews were permitted to "return" to Jerusalem and begin the reconstruction of the Temple. This was the beginning of both the physical and political *rebuilding*.

Drawing of Temple Construction by Gustave Dore

Incredibly, God has caused this edict to be preserved in the form an archeological artifact that even the secular world acknowledges. It is known as the *Cyrus Cylinder*, and it was discovered in 1879. The text of this amazing find describes how Cyrus "restored cult sanctuaries and repatriated deported peoples." This is exactly what his decree allowed the Jews to do — return to rebuild the Temple. It also includes these words:

83

"The Lord, the God of heaven has given me all the kingdoms of the earth" - Cyrus[20]

This is an exact word-for-word quote from Cyrus's decree in Ezra 1:1-2:

Thus says Cyrus King of Persia, **"The Lord, the God of heaven has given me all the kingdoms of the earth** *and He has appointed me to build Him a house in Jerusalem, which is in Judah."* (Ezra 1:2 NASB, emphasis mine)

After Cyrus's decree, an initial group of Jewish captives returned to Jerusalem and began reconstruction of the Temple. Unfortunately, after laying the foundation, the local gentile inhabitants of Palestine hindered the construction. In fact, they delayed the construction of the Temple until the reign of Darius the Great.

Then work on the house of God in Jerusalem ceased, and it was stopped until the second year of the reign of Darius king of Persia. (Ezra 4:24 NASB)

Therefore, the foundation of the Temple lay unfinished for years — during the entire reign of Cyrus, the entire reign of his son Cambysis II, and the short reign of Bardiya. In the Book of Ezra, these other kings are referred

---

[20] "The Persian Kings and Bible Chronology," *The Ensign Message*, last modified January, 2011, accessed April 9, 2018, http://ensignmessage.com/articles/the-persian-kings-and-bible-chronology/

to by their throne names, Ahasuerus and Artaxerxes (Ezra 4:6-7). The Bible indicates that those opposing the building sent letters to these kings asking them to stop the rebuilding. In their letters they implied that the Jews were more likely to revolt if the rebuilding of their city was completed (Ezra 4:6-24).

Then during the reign of Darius the Great a letter was sent to the king appealing to the original decree of Cyrus. Darius found Cyrus's decree and authorized the Temple construction to be completed (Ezra 6:1-12).

This brings us to the third of the four decrees by Persian kings, the decree of Artaxerxes I Longimanus in **457 BC** (Ezra 7:8-26). This decree allowed additional Jewish captives to return to Jerusalem from Babylon and provided Ezra with ample funds to complete the Temple beautification. He was also given sufficient funding to complete the construction of the city of Jerusalem started under the previous decrees. *This permitted the Jews to complete the command to* **rebuild** *Jerusalem.*

More importantly for our purposes here, this decree empowered Ezra and the Jews politically. First, it allowed Ezra to impose a tax on the gentile rulers in the provinces around Israel (Ezra 7:21-22 NASB). Second, this decree also empowered Ezra to implement Jewish law.

> *You, Ezra, according to the wisdom of your God which is in your hand, appoint magistrates and judges that they may judge all the people who are in the province beyond the River, even all those who know the laws of your God; and you may teach anyone who is ignorant of them. Whoever will not observe* **the law of your God** *and the law of the king, let judgment be executed upon him strictly, whether for death or*

for banishment or for confiscation of goods or for imprisonment. (Ezra 7:25-26 NASB, emphasis mine)

By means of this decree, the Jews were able to organize their government with magistrates and judges. They were also given the power of life and death. Most importantly, they were permitted to implement **Jewish law**. *This was the fulfillment of the command to* **restore** *Jerusalem to Israelite rule — completely consistent with our working theory.*

69 SHABUIM TO MESSIAH THE PRINCE

We have established that 69 sabbatical cycles of years **exactly** determine the time from the starting point (the decree) until the ending point (the baptism of Jesus). Let's look again at the graphic of the entire 70 Weeks to examine these starting and ending points more closely:

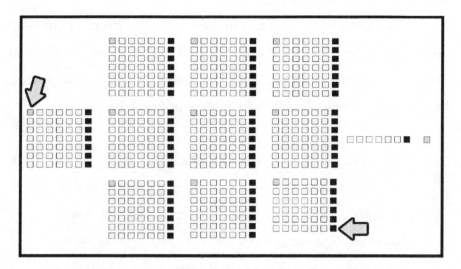

Figure 9: Sabbatical Years during 70 Shabuim

If AD 27 was truly the final year of the 69th Shabua, it was sabbatical year. The dark square representing this year is marked by a gray arrow on the right of the graphic. We have already discussed how Jesus's reading of a portion of Isaiah 61 in Luke 4 clearly indicated that the initial year of his ministry *was* a sabbatical year.

If this is correct, then looking back we can see that the first year (**457 BC**) was a Jubilee year. This year (a striped square) is marked by a gray arrow on the left of the graphic. There is evidence in the Book of Ezra to support 457 BC being a Jubilee year as there was a tax-exemption — but it was only for the priests (Ezra 7:24) — and a release of captives (Ezra 8:35), both being typical for a Jubilee Year. Additionally, because there would be no agricultural work during a Jubilee year, it makes sense that this was an ideal year for the exiles listed in Ezra 8 to make the four-month journey from Babylon to Jerusalem — they would not be needed in the fields, as the fields would lie fallow during that Jubilee year. There is also some consensus among Jewish scholars that this was the first Jubilee celebrated in Israel after the return from captivity.[21] Furthermore, if 457 BC was a Jubilee, a number of other important biblical events line up perfectly as Jubilee years as well (they are separated by multiples of 49 years).[22]

The year 457 BC as a Jubilee year makes complete sense because this year marked the beginning of the **ten Jubilee cycles** *of the entire 70 Weeks Prophecy. This supports our working theory – perfectly.*

---

[21] A. Strobel, Ursprung und Geschichte des Fruhchristlichen Osterkalenders [Texte und Untersuchungen, Band 121], pp. 92-95
[22] 163 BC – Maccabee revolt, 408 BC – completion of Jerusalem construction, 702 BC – God's miraculous destruction of the Assyrian army, and 947 BC – dedication of the first Temple. Interestingly, the dedication of the first Temple was 490 years (70 times 7) from the decree of Artaxerxes I. (Note: all ancient years are estimates)

PLAZA AND MOAT

The translated terms "Plaza and Moat" in the prophecy of Dan. 9:25 have additional insight for us.

The Hebrew word, *rechob*, means town "square." Ezra referred to this directly: *"All the people sat in the open **square** before the house of God"* (Ezra 10:9 NASB). The town square of Jerusalem appears to have been located directly in front of the Temple and served an important "political" purpose (remember our discussion of "to restore"). Legal decisions were made there (Ezra 10:9) and it was a place of instruction in the law (Neh. 8:1-3). It was also a place where justice was meted out (Isa 59:14).

The Hebrew word, *charuwts*, literally means "sharp pointed objects." Some think this noun means "wall," and some believe it means "moat." However, the verb-form of this word means "legal decision" (1 Ki. 2:40). In Joel 3:14, the noun-form is used in the famous phrase "valley of **decision**."

In combination, these two words present the idea of a courtroom (the square) and the legal decisions made there. *Again, this implies the political and legal development of the city of Jerusalem that was only instituted by **the decree of Artaxerxes in 457 BC**. And this, in turn, directly supports our working theory.*

THE REASON FOR THE DIVISION OF 7 AND 62 SHABUIM, AND THE "TIMES OF DISTRESS"

In Chapter Four, we discussed at length how the first seven Shabuim constituted a complete Jubilee cycle. One purpose God may have had for separating out the first Jubilee cycle was *to clearly and distinctly alert the Jews that the first year of the countdown was to be a Jubilee year* (see Figure 9). If the first century Jews were to be able to calculate the countdown, they needed to identify the starting point with absolute assurance. Starting with a Jubilee year helped to do that.

Second, by separating out a complete Jubilee cycle (the first seven Shabuim), *God left no doubt that the entire prophecy was about Jubilee cycles — ten of them.*

Finally, if our new theory is correct and the countdown began in 457 BC, the first seven Shabuim *after* the starting point would be completed in 408 BC. What significant events took place during the first 49 years, and what occurred in 408 BC?

First, these seven Shabuim were the transitions from Ancient Judaism to rabbinic Judaism. The Elephantine papyri tell us that 408 BC was the approximate date that the office of High Priest was established.[23]

Second, it is also considered a possible timing for the completion of the final book of the Old Testament, Malachi. In this way, this period marked the end of God's revelation to man until the coming of The Word himself, Jesus.

More importantly, it is also thought that the construction of Jerusalem was completed in 408 BC.[24] These 49 years during which the city was being completed were *times of distress* just as Dan. 9:25 informs us.

These times of distress are described for us in the Book of Nehemiah. One aspect of that Book, that will probably be a surprise to

---

[23] "A Chapter in the History of the High-Priesthood," *The American Journal of Semitic Languages and Literatures*, Vol. 55, No. 4 (Oct.,1938), pp. 360-377
[24] Humphrey Prideaux, *The Old and New Testament Connect in the History of the Jews*, Vol. I, p. 322

nearly everyone, is that the broken and burned walls of the city of Jerusalem that Nehemiah repaired was ***recent* damage**. The walls had already been repaired years before. When Ezra returned to Jerusalem in 457 BC, he saw the completed Temple and the completed wall:

> *For we are slaves; yet in our bondage our God has not forsaken us but has extended lovingkindness to us in the sight of the kings of Persia, to give us reviving to raise up the house of our God, to restore its ruins and to give us **a wall in Judah and Jerusalem**.* (Ezra 9:9 NASB, emphasis mine)

Prior to researching this book, I had always understood that Nehemiah repaired the walls originally destroyed by the Babylonians in 586 BC. But that is probably not correct and doesn't make sense. The passage above clearly shows that Ezra saw that wall in 457 BC. However, twelve years later in 445 BC, Nehemiah received this report:

> *I asked them concerning the Jews who had escaped and had survived the captivity, and about Jerusalem. They said to me, "The remnant there in the province who survived the captivity are in great distress and reproach, and the wall of Jerusalem is broken down and its gates are burned with fire."* **When I heard these words, I sat down and wept and mourned for days**.
> (Neh. 1:2-4 NASB, emphasis mine)

After hearing this, Nehemiah was *shocked and wept for days*. This was 445 BC — 141 years after the original destruction, 93 years after Cyrus's decree, and even 71 years after the Temple rebuilding was completed during the reign of Darius. Does it make sense that the Jews in Persia hadn't gotten news from Jerusalem for *seventy plus years* that the walls hadn't been repaired? No, the only logical answer is that this was *new* damage. **There obviously had been some sort of attack on the city.** These were the *times of distress* that Dan. 9:25 prophesied.

In addition, it only required fifty-two days for Nehemiah and the Jews to restore the walls (Neh. 6:15), while it took nearly four years to build a single building (the Temple). Doesn't it make sense that this was limited damage to the walls if it required such a short period to restore it? I think that makes sense.

THE "PROPHETIC YEAR"

This brings us to the fourth "so-called decree" of a gentile king, the letters of Artaxerxes in 445 BC. As we mentioned previously, *scripture never calls this a decree*. Nehemiah was granted letters to present to the governors of the provinces, but that is not a decree. And we already know that this cannot be the starting point of the 69 Shabuim, because the previous decree in 457 BC was both the starting point and a perfect 483 years to the anointing of the Messiah. But the fourth "so-called decree" *is* part of the prophecy; it is part of the first 49 years, the *times of distress*.

However, the majority of Christians today assume that these letters written in 445 BC are *the* prophetic decree. This thinking is based on the work of the earliest and most famous Christian author to propose an alternative length to the Shabuim, Scotland Yard Inspector Sir Robert Anderson. In his book *The Coming Prince (1894)*, he suggested that the 20th year of Artaxerxes was *the* decree to rebuild referenced in Dan. 9:25. However, he realized that the math did not work. Sixty-Nine Shabuim from this decree was the year AD 39, much too late to have anything to do with the coming of the Messiah. As a "work-around" to this problem, Anderson decided to create something called the "prophetic year" — a 360-day-year. He converted the 69 Shabuim of the prophecy into days (173,880 days) based on this new definition of a "year" formula. When he added this huge number of days to the date of the decree, he arrived at Palm Sunday, AD 32. Viola! Anderson thought he had solved the puzzle, and many still believe this to this day.

We have already discussed multiple reasons why alternative-length Shabuim cannot be correct. All of the reasons why the Shabuim must be traditional, Hebraic, solar/lunar years presented in Chapter Four (see pp. 42-56), contradict Anderson's theory.

Additionally, it is critical that the Shabuim be **actual years**, not some sort of mathematical construction based on a specific number of days. Only a year based on the interactions of the sun and moon is truly biblical as indicated in Gen. 1:14. Any year (such as a 360-day year) that is not based on the interaction of the sun and moon is not a biblically-based year.

This passage in Gen. 1 also informs us that God gave us the sun and moon for the *mo'edim* (appointed times) or Feasts of the Lord (Lev. 23). William Struse has pointed out that Jesus fulfilled the prophetic significance of all of the Spring Feasts of the Lord (Passover, Unleavened Bread,

Firstfruits, and Pentecost) using the traditional Hebraic solar/lunar calendar and not years based on a collection of a certain number of days.[25]

Finally, a theory based on a 360-day year violates the principle that God does nothing without first revealing it to his Holy Prophets (Amos 3:7). This type of Shabuim based on 360-day years is found nowhere in the Bible and would not have been understood by Daniel or the Jewish people.

In addition to all these reasons that discredit a 360-day year, AD 32, the year Anderson chose for the death of Messiah, is not a candidate year for the death and resurrection of Jesus! Nissan 14 (the day of the lamb's sacrifice) was a Monday that year, rather than a Friday (or even a Wednesday or Thursday according to some theories as to the day of Jesus's crucifixion).

Also, Anderson's calculation requires the utmost precision. In order to make it "work," he made an arbitrary decision. He chose the first day of the month of Nisan as his starting point even though the Bible gives only the month, not the day of the decree (Neh. 2:1). If the actual date of the decree was even a week later, his 69th week would end *after* the crucifixion not before it!

For all these reasons and more, *Anderson's theory is not biblical.* However, I fully realize that his formula is loved and cherished by millions of Christians world-wide, is utilized as a tool in apologetics, and is frequently applied in eschatology, where the 70th Shabua is considered to consist of two 1260-day periods. Unfortunately, based on the numerous proofs given, it is simply mistaken. I realize that giving up this theory may be very hard for many of you, but I suggest re-reading this section and the referenced

---

[25] William Struse, *Daniel's Seventy Weeks,* (PalmoniQuest LLC, 2015), loc. 2452

pages a couple times to allow the full weight of the evidence against Anderson's theory to sink in.

COUNTING THE YEARS TO MESSIAH

As we indicated at the beginning of this chapter, the first century Jew knew and understood the countdown. They were also carefully counting years in anticipation of it. In the first century, Jewish genealogies were carefully recorded and memorized so as to prove the genealogy of the Messiah when he came. Notice how the genealogy of Jesus is given in the Gospels of Matthew and Luke. So the Jews of that time were completely cognizant of the generations from the time of Daniel.

The concept that the first century Jews were counting years is also supported by the famous *Damascus Document* from the *Dead Sea Scrolls*. Its writer indicates that the Qumran Community was established 390 years after the Babylonian destruction of Jerusalem.[26] The Jews were counting years and aware of the number of years from each of the various decrees.

Additionally, the Jews almost certainly viewed the 70 Shabuim countdown as ten Jubilee cycles as we discovered from the evidence found in the *Melchizedek Pesher* from the *Dead Sea Scrolls*. Based on this understanding, they would have begun their countdown in a Jubilee year — 457 BC.

However, I assume that some were not completely convinced, and they began watching for potential messiahs to arrive on the scene at the end point of **each decree of the gentile kings** (Cyrus — 55 BC, Darius — 37

---

[26] Rendsburg, Gary A., The Dead Sea Scrolls (Great Courses, Chantilly, 2010), p.31

BC, Artaxerxes — AD 27 and AD 39). They also had no way of knowing if these years would be the birthdate or beginning of a kingly reign of the Messiah. As each end point passed with no true messiah, I assume they said to themselves, "Well, it wasn't that one, let's look for the next one."

And there were false messiahs. In the Book of Acts, Rabbi Gamaliel had this to say about false messiahs:

> *For some time ago* **Theudas** *rose up, claiming to be somebody, and a group of about four hundred men joined up with him. But he was killed, and all who followed him were dispersed and came to nothing. After this man,* **Judas of Galilee** *rose up in the days of the census and drew away some people after him; he too perished, and all those who followed him were scattered.* (Acts 5:35-37 NASB, emphasis mine)

Judas of Galilee was a potential messiah candidate in 4 BC.[27] Obviously, Theudas predated that era. Might these men have used the *70 Weeks Prophecy* and the end points of 55 BC or 37 BC to support their case for being the messiah? Perhaps.

We have already seen that in AD 27 the ministry of John the Baptist inspired the Jewish authorities to make messianic inquiries about him. Obviously, this date was correct as seen in hindsight, — Jesus was the Messiah. Unfortunately, they were blinded by sin and missed the Son of God.

---

[27] Jewish War 2.56 and Jewish Antiquities 17.271-272.

Did the Daniel 9 prophecy influence the Magi who visited Jesus when he was a toddler? They may have been aware that AD 27 was the most likely endpoint, and then assumed that a man beginning his reign as King of Kings at 30 years of age would be born about 3 BC. Is that why they watched the sky with special interest in that year? Perhaps so.

Which brings us to Josephus's statement that the 70 Weeks Prophecy was *the* determining factor in the Jewish revolt of AD 70. How might that have been? The latest potential endpoint of any of the Persian decrees was AD 39, which was 483 years after Artaxerxes' decree in 445 BC. In their understanding, this was the last chance for the prophecy to be fulfilled. There were no more decrees to use as assumed starting points.

If their messiah had been born in AD 39 (assuming the end point "to Messiah the Prince" meant his birth), he would have been about 30 years old in the year prior to AD 70. Since King David became king at 30 years of age and priests entered service at this same age, I assume the Jewish authorities felt this was the most likely time for a man born in AD 39 to begin his reign or ministry. (Jesus and John the Baptist both started their ministries at this same age.) So the Jews staked everything on their faith in their interpretation of the prophecy — and lost.

In the second century, the rabbis attempted to resurrect the *70 Weeks Prophecy* one more time to point *to* Bar Kokhbah and *away* from Jesus. Rabbi Akiva ben Joseph (writer of the Mishna) proclaimed Bar Kokhbah the Messiah, and in order to bolster Bar Kokhbah's standing, the Jews of that era reduced the number of suspected Persian kings in the chronology from 10 (extending over a period of 207 years) to 5 (extending over only 53 years). This move placed Cyrus's decree somewhere near the year 385 BC instead of 538 BC. Bar Kokhbah died in the Jewish revolt of AD 135 along with his messianic status, but the "missing" 154 years have permanently become part of the Jewish calendar[28] (although a total of 240 years are "missing" for various reasons).

Earlier in this chapter, we discussed many of the potential Jubilee years that are perfect 49-year multiples starting from 457 BC. I'd like to add one more — 132 AD. Bar Kokhbah's claim of messiah status was bolstered by the fact that his career probably began during a Jubilee year! The suspected date of the AD 132 Jubilee and its relation to the rise of "messianic fervor" is supported by Jewish historian Ben Zion Wacholder.[29] The discovery of a Jewish coin from Bar Kokhba's "reign" featuring twin Jubilee trumpets has added even more support — linking Bar Kokhba's "messianic" claim to the Jubilee.[30]

SUMMARY

Have we solved *Daniel's Mysterious Countdown*? I'm sure you'll agree the evidence is overwhelming. The command of God authorized the first three decrees of the Persian kings, starting with Cyrus in 538 BC and ending

---

[28] "The Jewish Calendar's Missing 240 Years," Prophecy in the News, last modified July 11, 2017, accessed Feb. 23, 2018, https://www.youtube.com/watch?v=qDzuf6SReSk

[29] Ben Zion Wacholder *Chronomessianism: The Timing Of Messianic Movements And The Calendar Of Sabbatical Cycles,* Hebrew Union College-Jewish Institute of Religion, Cincinnati, p217

[30] "NGC Ancients: The Coinage of Bar Kokhba," *NGC,* last modified Dec. 13, 2011, accessed April 24, 2018, https://www.ngccoin.com/news/article/2494/The-Coinage-of-Bar-Kokhba/

with Artaxerxes in 457 BC. These first three decrees of the Persian kings implemented God's command as it "went forth."

The countdown of 483 years "until Messiah the Prince" started in **457 BC** with the decree of Artaxerxes. This decree fulfilled the requirements for the start of the countdown of Daniel's prophecy, and the countdown concluded at Jesus's anointing at his baptism in **AD 27**.

The exact precision of this countdown is another testimony which we should share with those who don't believe. Jesus, indeed, literally fulfilled the messianic prophecy of Daniel and the counting of the 69 Shabuim when understood correctly.

I pray this humble book and the work presented here is influential in bringing to salvation as many saved souls as the Spirit intends. **Hosanna, Lord save. Amen.**

In the next chapter, we will begin to look at the significant events that happened after the 69 Shabuim countdown was completed.

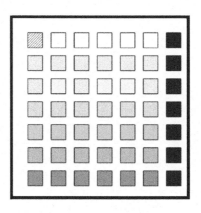

PART FOUR:

In the Gap

Chapter Seven

HISTORY OR FUTURE?

"And he will make a firm covenant with the many for one week, but in the middle of the week he will put a stop to sacrifice and grain offering; and on the wing of abominations will come one who makes desolate, even until a complete destruction, one that is decreed, is poured out on the one who makes desolate." (Dan. 9:27 NASB)

This Part Four of the book is entitled, "In the Gap", because it refers to the time between the 69th and 70th Shabuim of this prophecy. This is the time in which many prophecy experts believe we are now living, in the gap between the 69th Shabua – which ended prior to the crucifixion of Jesus — and before the 70th Shabua begins in the future.

However, as we've stated before, there is a very substantial movement in Christianity that believes the 70th Shabua was fulfilled in the first century, and that Daniel's *70 Weeks Prophecy* is entirely historic. In their minds, nothing in the final Shabua remains to be fulfilled.

This is such an important topic that we are devoting an entire chapter to its discussion. However, frankly, we shouldn't have to. Scripture directly proves that the entirely historic view is mistaken. The passage at the beginning of this chapter (Dan. 9:27) is found in the NASB and represents the English translation of the Hebrew Masoretic text. If we read *only* this text, Historicists may have some footing to present a case that the 70th Shabua is fulfilled. But this is not the only text.

The equally valid Greek Septuagint Old Testament indicates the 70th Shabua extends to the "end of time." This translation blows any thoughts of an already fulfilled 70th Shabua out of the water.

> *And one week shall establish the covenant with many: and in the midst*
> *of the week my sacrifice and drink-offering shall be taken away: and*
> *on the Temple shall be the abomination of desolations; and* **at the**
> **end of time** *an end shall be put to the desolation.*
> (Dan. 9:27 LXX, emphasis mine)

The Septuagint was the Old Testament text of the early Church. And based on comparison studies with the *Dead Sea Scrolls*, it appears to be just as valid as the Hebrew Masoretic text found in most English Bibles.[31] We cannot — and should not — ignore the LXX version of Dan. 9:27, which precludes an historic fulfillment of the 70th Shabua. But in the spirit of good exegesis, we will also examine the Hebrew text and see if it supports a futurist position as well.

AFTER THE 62 SHABUIM

We have seen that the majority of the *70 Weeks Prophecy* is a countdown "to Messiah the Prince." The two periods stated in Dan. 9:25 — 7 Shabuim and 62 Shabuim — add together to constitute this total 483-year countdown "to Messiah the Prince." Then we read what occurs after the 62 Shabuim:

---

[31] "Validity of LXX for Messianic Prophecy," *DOXA, Christian Thought in the 21st Century*, last modified unknown, accessed Feb. 9, 2018, http://www.doxa.ws/Messiah/Lxx_mt.html

*Then **after** the sixty-two weeks, the Messiah will be cut off and have nothing, and the people of the prince who is to come will destroy the city and the sanctuary. And its end will come with a flood; even to the end there will be war; desolations are determined. And he will make a firm covenant with the many for one week . . .*

(Dan. 9:26-27a NASB, emphasis mine)

After Gabriel explained the countdown to Daniel, he then clarified the five events that would take place after the coming of Messiah, the Prince.

- The Messiah would be "**cut off**" (i.e., crucified),

- The Messiah would "**have nothing**,"

- The people of the prince who is to come will **destroy the city and Temple**,

- There will be **war and desolations**, and

- A yet to be determined "he" will make **a covenant for one Shabua**, the final 70th Shabua.

Wow, Gabriel gave Daniel a lot of information in this verse and a half! From this information we can determine whether the 70th Shabua was an historic fulfillment in the first century, a future fulfillment, or both. So let's examine all of these aspects to see what we can learn from them.

The Messiah will be "Cut Off"

We already looked at this aspect of the prophecy in Chapter Three. There we learned that the Hebrew verb "cut off" is *karath* and is the same verb used in Gen. 15 where God "cut" the Abrahamic Covenant with Abraham and Israel. We learned that when God walked between the pieces of cut animals he was in essence communicating "if you (Israel) break this covenant, I will pay the price." This is the greatest one-sided deal in history — and praise God for it! Messiah the Prince being "cut off" is another way of saying Jesus died on the cross for the sins of the world.

Jesus addressed the material in Dan. 9:26 using several parables. The first of these was the *Parable of the Land Owner*, in Matt. 21:33-44. Jesus began the parable by quoting Isaiah's *Parable of the Vineyard* (Isa. 5:1-7), which likened Jerusalem to a vineyard. Jesus then entered his own parable as a character:

> But afterward he (the land owner) sent **his son** to them, saying, "They will respect my son." But when the vine-growers saw the son, they said among themselves, "This is the heir; come, let us kill him and seize his inheritance." **They took him and threw him out of the vineyard and killed him**. (Matt. 21:37-39 NASB, clarification and emphasis mine)

In this way, Jesus prophesied how he would be "cut off" (killed).

The Messiah will "Have Nothing"

The next phrase in Dan. 9:26 is quite unique and a bit hard to understand.

Then after the sixty-two weeks the Messiah will be cut off and **have nothing** (Dan. 9:26 NASB, emphasis mine)

Outmoded interpretations of this phrase ("*have nothing*") are cherished by some. Supersessionists (who believe all of God's promises made to Israel have been transferred to the Church) prefer to say that this phrase means the Jews will no longer be Jesus's people. This is *nonsense* because in Exodus 6:6-7 and in Jeremiah 31, God specifically prophesies about the future day when the Jews would become his people and he would become their God — *forever.*

The KJV beautifully renders the phrase "*have nothing*" as "but not for himself," implying that Jesus died for all. This is wonderful *and* true, but the KJV translation is considered to be a poor interpretation of the Hebrew.[32] The translation of the Hebrew idiom ("but not to") in the NASB is correct in my opinion. After being cut off, the Messiah will have nothing. What does this mean? What "nothing" will the Messiah have earned through his being cut off? This must refer back (have an antecedent) to something earlier in the prophecy.

I believe Dr. Thomas Ice, Director of the Pre-Trib. Research Center, correctly interprets this phrase. **Gabriel is telling us that Jesus will not have achieved all of the purposes of the** *70 Weeks Prophecy* (found in Dan. 9:24) with his crucifixion.[33] Rather, something more (the 70th

---

[32] "And have nothing," Pre-Trib. Research Center, last modified unknown, accessed Feb. 10, 2018, http://www.pre-trib.org/articles/view/daniel-926-and-have-northing
[33] Ibid.

Shabua) will be required to achieve all these goals, especially in relation to Daniel's people, Israel.

In and of itself, this phrase in the Hebrew also demonstrates that the *70 Weeks Prophecy* was not fulfilled in the first century. This is just common sense. All of Israel is not yet saved (Rom. 11:26). Something more is needed. And that something more is the 70th Shabua.

Christians are quick to misinterpret the cross and resurrection of Jesus as the completed Gospel as if nothing more is needed. Jesus began the work of Salvation on the cross, but his work won't be fully realized until his glorious Second Coming.

The Prince Who is to Come

Since all nine of the purposes of the 70 Shabuim were not accomplished solely at the cross (obviously many Jews are still apostate), Jesus began the unfinished work in the very next sentence in this verse.

> . . . *and the people of the prince who is to come will destroy the city and the sanctuary*. . . (Dan. 9:26 NASB)

From Dan. 9:26 we see that both the city of Jerusalem and the Temple that the Jews were relying on would be taken away.

If the last section is somewhat controversial, **this phrase about the coming prince is one of the most controversial passages in the entire Bible!** Who is the prince who is to come and who are his people? Why do they destroy the Temple? Dr. Thomas Ice, whom I believe was correct about the phrase "will have nothing" in the last section, has this to say:

"In the passage on the 70 weeks of Daniel, Gabriel tells Daniel that the anti-Christ will come from the same people who would destroy Jerusalem and the Temple, which happened in a.d. 70 (sic). Virtually everyone agrees that it was the Romans who achieved this destruction." — Thomas Ice[34]

This is the predominant — and most probably incorrect — view of the majority of Christians today. It assumes that the *"prince who is to come"* is the Antichrist, that the people of this prince are the same ethnicity as Antichrist, and that these people are the Romans. I disagree with Dr. Ice on all three points!

If we are going to tread on this opinion that some consider almost sacred, we need to do so cautiously. I would like to start by taking the discussion out of the realm of charged emotions and preconceived ideas and restate the first portion of the *70 Weeks Prophecy* as an allegory.

Seventy Weeks have been set aside for our community to bring it blessing. It will be 69 weeks to the long-awaited Taxpayer the Mayor. After the 69 weeks, the Taxpayer will

---

[34] "Will the Antichrist be a Muslim?" *Pre-Trib. Research Center*, last modified unknown, accessed Feb. 10, 2018, http://www.pre-trib.org/articles/view/will-the-anti-christ-be-a-muslim

be taxed but it won't accomplish everything. And the children of the Mayor who is to come will bulldoze the community, and then we'll all have to leave.

First of all, notice that the central figure in this allegory plays two roles, "Taxpayer" and "Mayor." At first, this may strike most readers as odd. But the ancient Jewish rabbis expected a Messiah with a dual nature, or even two separate Messiahs — a Messiah ben Joseph and a Messiah ben David. Raphael Patai who taught Hebrew at the Hebrew University of Jerusalem had this to say about the concept:

> When the death of the Messiah became an established tenet in Talmudic times, this was felt to be irreconcilable with the belief in the Messiah as Redeemer who would usher in the blissful millennium of the Messianic Age. The dilemma was solved by splitting the person of the Messiah in two: one of them, called Messiah ben Joseph, was to raise the armies of Israel against their enemies, and, after many victories and miracles, would fall victim [to] Gog and Magog. The other, Messiah ben David, will come after him (in some legends will bring him back to life, which psychologically hints at the identity of the two), and will lead Israel to the ultimate victory, the triumph, and the Messianic era of bliss. — Raphael Patai[35]

---

[35] Patai, Raphael, *The Messiah Texts*, Avon Books, © 1979, p. 166

Christians, of course, realize that these two roles of the Messiah are joined in one person — Jesus. He came first to suffer and then will return to reign as King. In the text of the *70 Weeks Prophecy*, these two roles are expressed by the Hebrew terms *mashiach* (Messiah) and *nagid* (prince or ruler), both found in the phrase *"Messiah the Prince"* in Dan. 9:25. In our allegory, these roles were "taxpayer" and "mayor."

Both of these terms, *mashiach* and *nagid*, are used again in the **very next verse**, Dan. 9:26. The *mashiach* is cut-off after which the people of the *nagid* destroy the city. So these are not two different persons, but the same person with a dual nature. Christians can grasp this easily because we are already aware of the two roles Jesus fills as Messiah and King.

The City and Temple Will be Destroyed

However, most Christians have missed the simple interpretation that the prince (*nagid*) of Dan 9:25 is the same person as the prince (*nagid*) in the very next verse, Dan. 9:26. One of the reasons that they may have missed this simple truth is that it is hard to consider the people of the Messiah as the ones who destroyed Jerusalem in AD 70. It is much easier to imagine the people of an evil prince destroying the city.

Jesus had a purpose in the destruction of Jerusalem and the Temple. Prior to his death and resurrection, Jews were able to deal with sin through a sacrificial system in which the blood of animals was poured out to cover their sins. However, after the Messiah was cut off for the sins of the whole world, the Temple was no longer required. Jesus permitted the Temple to stand for an additional forty-year period (AD 30 to AD 70), but he then allowed it to be destroyed.

The *Parable of the Wedding Feast* (Matt. 22:2-13) explains how the destruction of the Temple and city were to be accomplished under **Jesus's authority**:

> *But the king was enraged, and he sent his armies and destroyed those murderers and set their city on fire.* (Matt. 22:7 NASB, emphasis mine)

Notice that it is the king (Jesus) who sends *his* armies to burn the city. He may have allowed the destruction of Jerusalem and the Temple because they were hindering the apostate Jews' salvation. As long as they felt the Temple sacrifices were solving their "sin problem," they were less likely to accept the true solution — the Messiah who was cut off for their sins.

It is in his role as "Prince" (*"the prince that is to come"*) that Jesus commanded the destruction of the city and Temple. That same understanding is echoed in the Greek Septuagint:

> *He* [the Messiah] *shall destroy the city and the sanctuary with the prince that is coming* [Lit. "the one taking the lead, the one coming"]. (Dan. 9:26 LXX, clarification mine)

The Greek perfectly renders this thought. Jesus was going to destroy the city and Temple *with* the one that is coming. In this case that was Titus, the general of the Roman forces. Jesus destroyed the city using his agents, which just happened to be Titus and his soldiers. **It is also worth noting that in the *literal* Greek of verse 26, the term "prince" is not found**.

The People of the Prince

In addition, the Greek version of Dan. 9:26 doesn't contain any mention of the *"people of the prince."* This is problematic for those who try to claim this verse is *the* Scripture to prove a Roman Antichrist! As we have seen, the word "people" is incidental to the verse (it's not found in the LXX). And in the NASB, the "people" are those of Messiah the Prince, not the Antichrist. Regardless of which text one choses, Dan. 9:26 doesn't support a Roman Antichrist. However, since this is a difficult point, let's explore it further.

The historian Josephus records that a soldier in the Roman Legion "being hurried on by a certain divine fury" lit the Temple on fire through a "golden window."[36] The soldier's inclusion in the Roman Legion is the basis for the theory that the "people" of Dan. 9:26 were Romans.

Bible scholar Joel Richardson has done extensive research on this topic and concluded that although the soldiers in the Legions were citizens of Rome, they were made up of conscripts from many nations — and Syria in particular. In this manner, he concludes the "people" were likely to be ethnically Arab.[37]

Both of these groups, Italian Romans or Arabs, could be considered Jesus's "people" as well, who destroyed the city and Temple at his bidding. Josephus certainly credits the soldier's motive in setting the

---

[36] Josephus, War 6.4.5 249-253

[37] Joel Richardson, *Mideast Beast*, (WND Books, Washington, D.C. 2012), Chapter 7

Temple on fire to a supernatural or "divine" fury. This is consistent with both the *Parable of the Wedding Feast* and the LXX translation of Dan. 9:26.

Josephus presents an additional theory that is ignored by most scholars — that the Jews themselves (Jesus's *ethnic* people) were responsible for the destruction of the Temple. Although Josephus mentions the solider who lit the Temple on fire in a single sentence, he spends paragraphs explaining how at that time a Jewish civil war was taking place between the moderates (Pharisees) and the extremists (Zealots). The civil war resulted in both groups defiling of the Temple with the innocent blood of many who were killed *within* its confines.[38] This defilement and the war with Rome (which was not authorized by God) led to the Temple's destruction.

Josephus connects all of this to the *70 Weeks Prophecy*!

> For there was a certain **ancient oracle** of those men, that the city should then be taken and the sanctuary burnt, by right of war, when **a sedition should invade the Jews** and **their own hands should pollute the Temple** of God. Now, while these Zealots did not disbelieve these predictions, they **made themselves the instruments of their accomplishment**. — Josephus[39]

Josephus is obviously referring to Dan. 9:26 when he discusses the "ancient oracle." He also clearly implicates the apostate Jews as "instruments" of the

---

[38] Josephus, War 5.1.4 19-20
[39] Josephus, War 4.6.3 381-388

Temple's destruction. There is no question that in many ways Josephus is correct — the Jews brought the Temple's destruction upon themselves.

My personal opinion is that the *"people of the Prince* (Jesus)" included all of these races: Italians, Jews, and Arabs. In sin, the apostate Jews rejected their true Messiah, but they still trusted the *70 Weeks Prophecy*. As we learned in Chapter Six, they assumed AD 70 was the last possible date the prophecy could be fulfilled; and based on this faith, they revolted against Rome in hope that *their* Messiah would arise. Therefore, Jesus, the true Messiah, sent *his armies* (Matt. 22:7) made up of Arabs and Italians to destroy the city that rebuffed him. He did this so that eventually they might accept him.

The "people of the Prince" (Jews, Arabs, and Italians) destroyed the city and the sanctuary just as the angel Gabriel prophesied.

The major take-away from this analysis is that Dan. 9:26 is not a proof text for the ethnicity of the Antichrist — be it Roman, Arab, or Jew. The *70 Weeks Prophecy* mentions his ethnicity; however, it does so in Dan. 9:27. We will discuss this aspect of the prophecy in Chapter Nine.

A Flood and War

We are told that the destruction of the city and Temple will come with a flood of wrath:

> . . . *And its end will come with a flood; even to the end there will be war; desolations are determined.* (Dan. 9:26 NASB)

The Jews of the first century who refused to acknowledge the Messiah also refused the New Covenant in his blood. Instead they chose a covenant that led to death:

> *Because you have said, "We have made a* **covenant with death**, *and with Sheol we have made a pact. The overwhelming* **scourge (lit. flood)** *will not reach us when it passes by, for we have made falsehood our refuge and we have concealed ourselves with deception." Therefore, thus says the Lord God, "Behold, I am laying in Zion a stone, a tested stone, A costly cornerstone* (Jesus) *for the foundation, firmly placed. He who believes in it will not be disturbed."* (Isa. 28:15-16 NASB, clarification and emphasis mine)

Because the Jews trusted in a *covenant* with death and not in the trusted cornerstone, who is Jesus (Acts 4:11), the flood of God's wrath came and swept their Temple away by means of a war with the Romans.

Desolations are Decreed

The final phrase of this verse is that "desolations are determined (or decreed)." What desolation is Gabriel talking about? We know that after the destruction of AD 70 (and in the later Bar Kokhba revolt in AD 132-134) , the Jewish people were driven out of Israel and scattered among the nations for nearly 1900 years. This strangely echoes the desolations that God prescribed as punishment for breaking the Mosaic Covenant:

And I will scatter you among the nations, and I will unsheathe the sword after you, and your land shall be a desolation, and your cities shall be a waste. (Lev. 26:33 NASB)

The 70 years of exile in Babylon were the result of the breaking of the Mosaic Covenant. We discussed this in Chapter Three. In Lev. 26, God laid out the initial punishment:

But if you will not listen to me and will not do all these commandments, if you spurn my statutes, and if your soul abhors my rules, so that you will not do all my commandments, but break my covenant, then I will do this to you . . . (Lev. 26:14-16 NASB)

The next few verses that follow Lev. 26:14–16 outline God's punishment.

We also know that by his grace and mercy God ended the 70 years of exile to Babylon in fulfillment of the prophecy given in Jeremiah. The *70 Weeks Prophecy* was an answer to the exile; a rebuilding of the ancient ruins and a return to Israel. However, the ominous ending to Dan. 9:26 seems to indicate that *more* desolations were in store for the Jewish people because of their rejection of the cornerstone, Jesus.

If we return to Lev. 26 and the section about God's punishment for Israel's disobedience, we see an incredibly stern follow-up warning that comes after his initial punishment. Four times, he makes a statement similar to this:

> *But if in spite of this you will not listen to me, but walk contrary to me, then I will walk contrary to you in fury, and I myself will discipline you **sevenfold** for your sins.* (Lev. 26: 27-28 NASB, emphasis mine)

In this passage, God states that he will punish Israel *sevenfold* for their *continual* disobedience and he repeats this warning four more times in this section (Lev. 26:18,21,24,28). If God initially punished Israel with 70 years of exile, a *sevenfold* exile punishment would be 70 times 7 or 490 years. Four of these *sevenfold* exiles would total 1960 years. Were these the desolations that were decreed to take place *after* the Jews rejected the Jesus? After AD 70, the Jews were scattered among the nations for 1878 years before Israel was restored in 1948. Although many Jews are back in the land, not all of them are; and the vast majority are still walking in rejection of Jesus.

I am *not* a date setter. However, might the year AD 2030 hold some significance (AD 70 plus 1960 years of exile)? Perhaps it does, perhaps it doesn't. One thing we can say for certain, however, is that the Jews were exiled from Israel for an amazingly long duration while the land remained desolate. And we can probably say with certainty that this was a desolation that was decreed.

HISTORY OR FUTURE?

In summary, we find that the four events that Dan. 9:26 outlines for us (the crucifixion, the Messiah having nothing, the destruction of the city and Temple, and the subsequent desolation of Jerusalem) point to a **future** seven-year period— the 70 Shabua of Daniel — and not to a historic fulfillment only. In the text, these four events are found *after* the 69th Shabua and prior to the 70th Shabua. This is evidence that they take place "in the gap," just as they are found in the text. To say otherwise is to "stretch" the meaning of the passage.

In addition, we find five other proofs for a future 70th Shabua of Daniel:

- Daniel's prayer and allusion to the Abrahamic Covenant in Dan. 9:4 was a prayer for the restoration of the land. This did not happen in the first century. Rather a desolation ensued of almost 1900 years. The final answer to Daniel's prayer for fulfillment of the Abrahamic Covenant will be at the end of the 70th Shabua,

- The phrase "have nothing" certainly seems to indicate that none of the goals of the *70 Weeks Prophecy* were completely fulfilled upon the death of Messiah,

- The fact that the death of Messiah and the eventual destruction of the Temple are grouped into a single set of events *after* the first 69 Shabuim and *prior* to the 70th Shabua, seems to indicate that they were to occur "in the gap" between these Shabuim.

- Gabriel's mention of the destruction of the Temple in AD 70 and the desolations that followed it are an indication to us that the purposes of the *70 Weeks Prophecy* were incomplete at that point. Gabriel only included the details of this future destruction because it was *related* to the prophecy. If it wasn't, and if the purposes of the prophecy had been fulfilled prior to the Temple's destruction,

Gabriel would have ended the prophecy with the death of Messiah and never included information about the Temple.

- As we indicated in Chapter Four, in Matt. 18:21-22, Jesus indicates that we are to forgive others up until — but not after — the end of 70 Shabuim, which precludes a Historicist position

In **Part Five,** we will examine the mysterious 70th Shabua of Daniel's Prophecy. In that study we will uncover additional proofs that the Historicist position is not tenable.

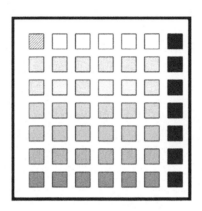

PART FIVE:

THE 70TH SHABUA OF DANIEL

Chapter Eight

THE COVENANT WITH THE MANY

And he shall make a strong covenant with many for one week, and for half of the week he shall put an end to sacrifice and offering . . . (Dan. 9:27 NASB)

In the first chapter of this book, we asked the question, "What is the most significant prophecy in the Bible?" No less a voice than John Walvoord responded:

> The interpretation of the revelation given to Daniel concerning the seventy weeks (Dan. 9:24-27) constitutes one of the determining factors in the whole system of prophecy. — John Walvoord[40]

And the final verse of the *70 Weeks Prophecy*, Dan. 9:27, the one that is yet future, is the aspect that frames our system of prophecy as Walvoord states. Yet despite the importance of this prophecy, it is greatly misunderstood. Much of that misunderstanding centers on the half-verse of Dan. 9:27a quoted above. There are two main schools of thought on what this half-verse means.

The **Historicist Position** believes that the 70th shabua was an historic event which included the ministry of Jesus (3 ½ years in their opinion), the

[40] "The Seventieth Week of Daniel," Bible.org, last modified unknown, accessed February 3, 2018, https://bible.org/seriespage/chapter-5-seventieth-week-daniel

crucifixion which ended the need for sacrifices, and a final 3 ½ years during which the Church developed. In their opinion, the Covenant with the many that is mentioned was the **New Covenant** Jesus ratified with his blood on the cross.

The **Traditional Futurist Position** believes that the 70th Shabua has not occurred yet. Their opinion is that the Covenant with the many is a peace treaty between the Antichrist and Israel. They further assume that the Antichrist breaks the peace treaty at the midpoint of the seven-year period and ends sacrifice and offerings in a rebuilt Jewish Temple.

Although there may be nuances to these two main positions, there really hasn't been a **third position** on what this half-verse means — until now. It is my opinion that both camps have misinterpreted this half-verse to the detriment of their followers. If we misunderstand the verse that constitutes the framework upon which we build the rest of our end time theories, we truly have done a disservice to the Word.

So, let's look at each of the positions and see why I believe **another** interpretation of Dan. 9:27 is needed.

THE HISTORICIST POSITION

The Historicist camp believes that Jesus is the "he" that makes a covenant with the many in this half-verse, Dan. 9:27a. They correctly observe that "he" requires an antecedent, a clearly identified name to which it refers. As we learned in the previous chapter, this is *Messiah the Prince*, whose people destroyed the City and the Temple just as prophesied in the *Parable of the*

122

Wedding Feast in Matt. 22:7. The Antichrist isn't mentioned in the *70 Weeks Prophecy* at all prior to the use of "he" in verse 27.

Unfortunately, in my opinion, that is about all the Historicist camp gets right. We will look at each aspect of this verse and see why an Historicist position is impossible. The proofs that follow add to the five proofs provided at the end of the previous chapter. In total, this evidence should eliminate the Historic position from your consideration as you reflect on which position is most valid.

He Will Strengthen a Covenant, not Make One

The Historicist camp claims that the covenant Jesus makes with the many is the **New Covenant** ratified by his blood on the cross. Unfortunately for this position, this is not what the original languages state. The word translated "make" is the Hebrew *gabar*. In the Greek, the equivalent word is *dynamoo`*. Both words carry a meaning of strengthening or empowering. *Therefore, Jesus doesn't "make" a New Covenant with the many, he strengthens a pre-existing covenant.*

Some **Historicists** claim that Jesus strengthened the **Mosaic Covenant** and the **New Covenant** was the result. However, the **New Covenant** is, by its very definition, a "new" covenant, and it is not a revised or strengthened version of any older covenant — for example, the **Mosaic Covenant**.

The specific language in Dan. 9:27a about the strengthening of a covenant precludes the **Historicist** position.

He Strengthens the Covenant for only One Shabua

The Historicist camp is also at a loss as to why both the Hebrew and Greek texts claim the Covenant is strengthened for only one Shabua. The New Covenant is an everlasting covenant. Certainly, if this verse was speaking of it, the verse would say, "He will make an everlasting covenant with the many." However, the verse is clear that the strengthening of the covenant is for only one shabua.

He Puts an End to Sacrifice and Offerings

One of the attractive aspects of the Historicist position is the elimination of sacrifices and offerings at the midpoint of the Shabua. Jesus's once-for-all sacrifice upon the cross certainly made the Hebraic sacrificial system unnecessary. In fact, it made it blasphemous. To trust in the blood of goats and sheep rather than the Holy blood of the Messiah is a grave sin. However, Jesus's death on the cross did not end or eliminate these sacrifices in the Temple. Apostate Jews continued to make sacrifices for forty more years. The destruction of the Temple in AD 70 eliminated them. It is impossible to imagine any length of Shabuim that would include Jesus's death and the destruction of the Temple 40 years later (which would only be the midpoint of this enormous 80-year Shabua).

In the Septuagint, we are given an additional nuance of understanding about the elimination of sacrifice:

> . . . *in the midst of the week my sacrifice and drink-offering shall be* **taken away***.* (Dan. 9:27 LXX, emphasis mine)

In the Greek text, we observe that the sacrifices and offerings are "taken away" by someone other than "he." This is absolutely inconsistent with an Historicist position that claims Jesus made these sacrifices unnecessary. No one else could have made the first-century sacrifices unnecessary, only Jesus's death (according to Historicist understanding) could have done so. Therefore, the Septuagint again refutes the Historicist position.

In the "Middle of the Week" Requires a 3 ½ Year Ministry of Jesus

In order for the Historicist position to have merit, it requires that Jesus's ministry be *exactly* 3 ½ years long. The Gospel accounts can be contorted to support this length of ministry, but there is no solid proof for it. Based on historical dates, the most likely length of Jesus's ministry was 2 ½ to 3 years (AD 27 to AD 30).

THE SEMI-HISTORICIST POSITION

There is a position related to the **Historicist Position** which assumes only the first half of the 70th Shabua was fulfilled by Jesus in the first century. At that point they suppose that a 2000-year gap then occurred, and that the second half of the Shabua will be fulfilled in the future.

This **Semi-Historicist Position** favors a future time of trouble that is only 1260 days long, rather than a full seven years. In defense of this position, proponents show that the New Testament only refers to periods of 1260 days, the famous "time, times, and half a time," or 42 months, when referencing the future time of trouble.

Although this position is more tenable than the **Historicist Position**, all the proofs against the **Historicist Position** in *this chapter* apply to this position as well. Dan. 9:27 does not apply to the first century, either in whole or in part.

In conclusion, in these last two chapters we have now presented a total of nine proofs that the 70th Shabua is not an historic event but, rather, a future one. If you wish to refresh your memory, these nine proofs may be found on pages 116-117 and 123-125.

THE TRADITIONAL FUTURIST POSITION

The Traditional position is a futurist position. Those who favor this position believe that the "he" in Dan. 9:27 refers to the coming Man of Sin, the Antichrist. They further believe that he will negotiate a future peace covenant with Israel and terminate their sacrifices in a yet to be built Temple of God at the Midpoint of the 70th Shabua.

As we have just demonstrated by our nine proofs, the Traditional Futurist Position is correct that the 70th Shabua is a future event. Unfortunately for this position, however, they are mistaken about the identity of the "he" in Dan. 9:27. They mistakenly claim that it is the Antichrist; the majority of the Church is therefore watching for a peace treaty with Israel to be "the" sign that the 70th Shabua has begun. This is a critical mistake. If the Church is watching for the wrong sign, it may be deceived.

"He" Will Make a Covenant

As we discussed previously, the pronoun "he" in Dan. 9:27 requires an antecedent. It requires a name previously mentioned in the text to clarify the identity of the person being referenced. The antecedent is usually the last clearly-identified name in the text prior to the pronoun. The Traditional Futurist community has looked at Dan. 9:26 and said, "The 'prince who is to come' is the last clearly identified name."

> *And after the sixty-two weeks, an anointed one shall be cut off and shall have nothing. And the people of* **the prince who is to come** *shall destroy the city and the sanctuary . . . And he will make a firm covenant with the many for one week.* (Dan. 9:26-27 NASB, emphasis mine)

There is a great deal of controversy about what the true antecedent to "he" is in this passage — whether it is the Messiah or the prince who is to come. *If they are the same individual (Jesus), this argument doesn't matter.* As we demonstrated in the previous chapter, the word *nagid* (prince) is associated with the Messiah, the Lord Jesus himself. **This is an overwhelming proof**. Whichever side of this argument about antecedents you prefer, Jesus is the answer since *he is both Messiah and Prince.*

Even if one rejects the elaborate proof in the previous chapter that the "prince who is to come" is Jesus, there is still absolutely no basis to ascribe this term to the Antichrist. The people of this prince destroyed the Temple in AD 70. If one rejects that Jesus is the prince, then Titus, the general in command of the Roman legion, would be considered the prince. There is absolutely no basis to assign that role to the Antichrist because he had nothing to do with the destruction of the city and Temple.

Finally, we will briefly mention a third argument which we will explain in more detail in the next chapter. The Antichrist *is* mentioned in the *70 Weeks Prophecy* —but in verse 27, not in verse 26. He is termed "one who makes desolate" and is contrasted with the "he" who strengthens the covenant. **The Antichrist can't be both.** Additionally, he is said to "come" or is revealed on the wings of abomination *after* the midpoint of the Shabua, not for the full Shabua, as necessary for a 7-year covenant.

I realize that this interpretation is contrary to what is taught throughout 99% of the Church. But if we're wrong about who "he" is in Dan. 9:27, then we will be watching and expecting the wrong things and be deceived.

The "he" who makes or strengthens the Covenant with the many can only be the Lord Jesus, our Messiah.

Does this mean the Antichrist won't negotiate a peace treaty with Israel? No, it doesn't mean that at all. What it means is that any peace treaty he is involved with is *not* the sign that the 70th Shabua of Daniel has begun. A peace treaty can begin prior to the 70th Shabua (most likely) or after it is already in progress.

In Jesus's great end time teaching, the Olivet Discourse, he confirms that we are not to watch for a peace treaty as a sign that the 70th Shabua has begun. In this great sermon on the 70th Shabua, the disciples initiated the conversation with this question:

> *The disciples came to Him privately, saying, "Tell us, when will these things happen, and what will be the sign of your coming, and of the end of the age?"* (Matt. 24:3 NASB)

This is the same question many of us have about end times. "What will be the sign of Jesus's coming?" This was the perfect opportunity for Jesus to say, "When you *see* the Antichrist negotiate his peace treaty . . ." However, that's not what he said.

> *And Jesus answered and said to them, "See to it that no one misleads you."* (Matt. 24:4 NASB, emphasis mine)

Instead, Jesus warned them about deception. The sign that the 70th Shabua will have already begun comes later in the discourse.

> *Therefore, when you* **see** *the* **abomination of desolation** *which was spoken of through Daniel the prophet, standing in the holy place [let the reader understand]* (Matt 24: 15 NASB, emphasis mine)

The *Abomination of Desolation* is the first clear sign that Jesus instructs his followers to *see*. And interestingly, notice that it is in reference to the prophet Daniel (and the *70 Weeks Prophecy!*) Therefore, Jesus doesn't expect his followers to clearly see and understand that they are in the 70th Shabua until the midpoint is upon them (when the *Abomination of Desolation* takes place).

In the Olivet Discourse, Jesus does give his disciples other signs prior to the *Abomination of Desolation*: deception by false messiahs, wars and rumors of war, famine, and earthquakes. But, these signs can be generalized. We have had false messiahs, wars, famine and earthquakes for the last 2000 years. We could easily miss signs like that. Jesus gave us a distinct sign to look for: The *Abomination of Desolation* which we will discuss in the next chapter.

He also clearly did *not* say we are to watch for the Antichrist's peace treaty. In fact, Jesus didn't mention a peace treaty at all.

The Abomination of Desolation in the middle of the 70th Week is the first clear sign that Jesus instructs his followers to see — not a prior peace treaty.

"He" Strengthens a Seven-Year Covenant

I'm sure our discussion in the previous sections are sufficient for you to see that the Antichrist's peace treaty is not being discussed in Dan. 9:27. However, if the previous sections weren't enough, also consider the following facts.

First, if the Covenant in Dan. 9:27 was referring to a peace treaty, it would have to be an existing treaty since it is "strengthened" (*gabar*). Some have recognized this fact and suggested that it is the Oslo Accords or another existing treaty involving Israel that the Antichrist strengthens.

Second, also consider that he has to strengthen this treaty for exactly seven years; not more and not less. It must last this *precise* period of time. Some will claim that the treaty begins on the first day of the 70th Shabua and Jesus terminates it on the last day when he returns, but this is impossible. Any peace treaty would be broken at the midpoint, when the Antichrist invades Israel, as stated in Luke 21:20-24. Most Traditional Futurists also believe that revived Jewish sacrifices will be part of the treaty. Both the sacrifices and the peace will end at the midpoint, so it is almost impossible to conceive that this treaty lasts for exactly seven years.

"He" Ends the Sacrifice and Offerings

The wording of Dan. 9:27 indicates that the "he" who strengthens the covenant is also the "he" who brings the revived Jewish sacrifices to an end. Traditional Futurists will argue that it is the Antichrist, not Jesus, who does this.

However, as we saw in our discussion of the **Historicist Position**, the Septuagint is quite clear that the sacrifices and drink offerings are "taken away." Both can be true. Jesus can authorize or permit the Antichrist to take away the sacrificial system. The Antichrist can be Jesus's agent to accomplish his will. As we discussed before, the sacrificial system is a crutch for the unsaved Jews, allowing them to believe that they are righteous when they aren't. The removal of this system of animal sacrifices causes them to realize their sin and seek the only real solution: Jesus.

THE FUTURIST-SPIRITUAL POSITION

If neither the **Historicist** nor **Traditional Futurist Positions** are correct, we need to propose a third theory — one in which Jesus strengthens the Covenant. But how is it that Jesus strengthens a covenant? What covenant is it, and how does Jesus accomplish this? And why is it only strengthened for seven years?

I have termed this newly theorized position the **Futurist-Spiritual Position,** because as we examine these questions we are forced to view the 70th Shabua of Daniel from the perspective of God's purposes — his spiritual purposes.

"He" Strengthens a Covenant

Our discussion thus far in this chapter has clearly shown that the "he" that strengthens the Covenant in Dan. 9:27 is the Lord Jesus. This strengthening is for one Shabua only and happens in the final seven years before the end of time.

If these characteristics are true — and at this point I assume you'll agree that they are — then we are in new territory. To the best of my understanding, **this theory has not been suggested before**. Let's examine the implications of it.

First, what Covenant is Jesus strengthening for one and only one Shabua? There are only four choices: the **Abrahamic**, the **Mosaic**, the **Davidic**, and the **New Covenant**. We discussed these covenants in chapter three. We also need to answer the question of *how* Jesus strengthens the Covenant.

Let's look at the **Davidic Covenant** first. God will fulfill the Davidic Covenant at the end of the 70th Shabua. But does he strengthen it during the Shabua? I'd have to say, "No." Jesus is sitting upon the throne of his Father for the majority of the Shabua. Only at the very end does he return to the earth and sit upon David's Throne, his glorious throne (Rev. 3:21). Therefore, it isn't the Davidic Covenant that is strengthened.

Let's consider the **Mosaic Covenant** next. God superseded the Mosaic Covenant with the superior **New Covenant** upon the death and resurrection of Jesus. The old sacrificial system of the Mosaic Covenant didn't ever really take away sins (Heb. 10:1-4); it simply looked forward to Jesus who would be the perfect sacrifice (Heb. 9:11-28). The unsaved Jews during the 70th Shabua will more than likely try to re-institute the sacrificial system and renew the Mosaic Covenant. Could this be the "strengthening of a Covenant" mentioned in Dan. 9:27?

I don't think so. Consider that the sacrifices are terminated half-way through the Shabua, but the text of the Daniel passage says that the covenant is strengthened for the *entire* Shabua. Also, consider that it is Jesus who does the strengthening. Would Jesus actually desire to strengthen the Mosaic Covenant, a covenant that was considered inferior, one that he died to replace with the New Covenant? It's doubtful.

Third, let's consider the **Abrahamic Covenant**. The terms of the Abrahamic Covenant are many. God promised the land to Abraham's descendants. This won't occur during the 70th Shabua, but at the completion of it. God also promised Abraham many descendants and this has already been fulfilled in abundance. You and I are spiritually children of Abraham.

Finally, God promised to bless all the nations of the earth through Abraham's seed, who is Jesus. This is an ongoing blessing. In the 70th Shabua, a final fulfillment of that blessing will take place when the Messiah lands upon the earth and all of Israel is saved. However, this is also not something that takes place for the entire Shabua.

No, none of these Old Testament covenants really provide a definitive match with Dan. 9:27. The only option remaining is that God strengthens the **New Covenant**.

The New Covenant is Strengthened

How does one strengthen an already great Covenant? When I began to search out the meaning of this phrase, I had the same question, "How can you improve on the **New Covenant**?" Obviously when someone is saved, they are saved. No one can be saved to a greater degree. And why would the Covenant only be strengthened for one Shabua? We need to answer both questions.

In order to understand this concept, we'll explore the Old Testament roots of the New Covenant. God gave the old, **Mosaic Covenant** to Moses who foresaw that the Jewish people would falter and not keep it. Moses also foresaw a day when God would give them a **New Covenant** that would change their hearts and make them want to obey and serve him. (Deut. 30:1-5)

Jeremiah was later given a vision of this **New Covenant** to come as well and spoke of a changed heart, a new creation. "*I will put My law within* *them and on their heart, I will write it; and I will be their God, and they shall be My people"* (Jer. 31:33 NASB).

Ezekiel also foresaw the coming **New Covenant** written upon the hearts of Israel.

> *Moreover, I will give you a new heart and put a new spirit within you; and I will remove the heart of stone from your flesh and give you a heart of flesh. I will put* **My Spirit within you** *and cause you to walk in My statutes.* (Ezek. 36:26-27 NASB, emphasis mine)

Ezekiel adds what the other prophets implied, that the Holy Spirit would indwell God's people with a new heart.

However, there is a problem. These prophetic visions show all of Israel living under the New Covenant *after* the Second Coming of the Messiah, after they are freed from the captivity of Antichrist and are living in their own land. So how can the **New Covenant** be strengthened for the entire 70th Shabua? It certainly isn't strengthened for the apostate Jews.

The only possible answer is that the New Covenant is strengthened for the Church. The <u>Church</u>, which includes the Jews who have come to Christ, is the "many" in Dan. 9:27.

Now that we understand it is the **New Covenant** that is strengthened, we still must resolve *how* it is strengthened.

> *It will come about after this that I will pour out My Spirit on all mankind; And your sons and daughters will prophesy, your old men will dream dreams, your young men will see visions.*
> (Joel 2:28 NASB)

This passage is found in an obvious end time context in Joel 2. Most scholars have rightly assumed that it discusses a coming of the Holy Spirit to the lost Jews to enable them to cry out, *"Blessed is he who comes in the Name of the Lord,"* to bring back their Messiah Jesus. God will empower them in this way. However, that happens toward the end of the 70th Shabua.

What if this passage also gives a hint of what God plans to do for those already under the **New Covenant** during the entire 70th Shabua? The Church is currently in-dwelt by the power of the Spirit. But there is a difference between that and the pouring out of his Spirit in excess on believers, much like Acts 2:4, when they spoke in numerous other languages. Interestingly, Peter quotes Joel 2:28 in his sermon on Pentecost in Acts 2! Is an Acts 2 type of empowering of the Spirit in store for the future 70th Shabua Church? It may well be.

Empower is an interesting word. It is a primary meaning of *dynamoo* in the Greek text of Dan. 9:27, the Old Testament text read by the early Church. The literal rendering of the Greek in this passage is, "And he will *empower* the Covenant for many for one period of sevens."

In the New Testament, both other uses of this Greek word, *dynamoo`*, carry this meaning of empowering by the Holy Spirit. The use in Hebrews — from the section known as the "Hall of Faith" in Chapter 11 — is incredibly insightful and relevant to the 70th Shabua:

> *Who by faith conquered kingdoms, performed acts of righteousness, obtained promises, shut the mouths of lions, quenched the power of fire, escaped the edge of the sword, from weakness* **were made strong (lit. empowered: dynamoo`)**, *became mighty in war, put foreign armies to flight. Women received back their dead by resurrection; and others were tortured, not accepting their release, so that they might obtain a better resurrection; and others experienced mockings and scourgings, yes, also chains and imprisonment. They were stoned, they were sawn in two, they were tempted, they were put to death with the sword.* (Heb. 11:33-37 NASB, emphasis mine)

Is the writer of Hebrews discussing the Old Testament or the coming Great Tribulation? Obviously, it is the Old Testament by context. But this portion of Scripture reads like it's right out of one of our Christian culture's "Tribulation" movies. And the Spiritual empowerment demonstrated in those types of faith-acts is precisely the meaning of the word *dynamoo`* found in Dan. 9:27. Whoever is empowered in this way receives spiritual dynamite (the word "dynamite" is derived from *dynamoo`*).

IMPLICATIONS FOR THE 70ᵀᴴ SHABUA CHURCH

The first and most obvious implication is that **the Church will be present during the 70ᵗʰ Shabua**. If God plans to empower many who are living under the **New Covenant** for the 70ᵗʰ Shabua, they will be there from the start. I realize this is an extremely uncomfortable thought for many who are planning to be whisked away to safety before any hard times begin.

However, read the passage in Hebrews again. What is God's reaction to those in this "Hall of Faith?" Don't you think God is enormously pleased with them? Is God going to give this job of being great heroes of the faith during the 70th Shabua to another people? Or is he going to call on his Church, his chosen people, his chosen priesthood to rise up and be empowered like that?

I realize this is an emotional and sensitive subject, and it may seem a bit far afield from our discussion about the *70 Weeks Prophecy*. I have written two other books on this subject. One is more easily understood, and one is more broad and complex; but both present the evidence for the timing of the various Rapture timing theories (pretrib., prewrath, or post-trib.) in a highly-organized way. If you are open-minded enough to seek the biblical answer, I think you will find it in these books:

Simplifying the Rapture (Ready for Jesus Publications, Wilmington, 2018)

Rapture: Case Closed? (Ready for Jesus Publications, Wilmington, 2017)

Drawing of the coming of the Holy Spirit by Gustave Dore

The second implication of the empowering of the Covenant is that this depiction presents the Church in the midst of the 70th Shabua in a way that is probably the exact opposite of what you have long-imagined. Perhaps you have envisioned Christians hiding in bunkers, eating beans, and concealing themselves from the forces of the Antichrist. In contrast, the **Futurist-**

Spiritual Position imagines a "hero" Church, empowered by the Holy Spirit to perform great acts of faith and courage during the 70th Week.

The words given to Daniel in another vision, during the third year of Cyrus, seem to echo the passage in Hebrews:

> *But the people who know their God will display strength and take action. Those who have insight among the people will* **give understanding to the many***; yet they will fall by sword and by flame, by captivity and by plunder for many days . . . Those who have insight will shine brightly like the brightness of the expanse of heaven, and those who* **lead the many to righteousness***, like the stars forever and ever.* (Dan. 11:32-34, Dan. 12:4 NASB, emphasis mine)

Notice that the *purpose* of the empowering faith is to lead many to righteousness. The Church will enter the 70th Shabua in order to testify, both by their words and by their sacrificial deeds. The word "testimony" is found in the Olivet Discourse accounts of Matt., Mark, and Luke, and *nine* (9) times in Revelation.

> **Testimony, empowered by the Holy Spirit, is the purpose of the Church in the 70th Shabua**

In this chapter, the meaning of the second half of the subtitle of this book, **the Church's Heroic Future**, becomes apparent. Who doesn't want to be a great hero of the faith for Jesus? Can you see how our misunderstanding of the *70 Weeks Prophecy* has led to a vastly misinterpreted understanding of the Church's future destiny and mission?

In the next chapter, we will examine the remainder of Dan. 9:27 and uncover more insights into mysteries. We will also reveal additional ways in which the Historicist and Traditional Futurist Positions are inconsistent with the biblical record.

Chapter Nine

THE ABOMINATION AND THE DESOLATOR

On the wing of abominations will come one who makes desolate, even until a complete destruction, one that is decreed, is poured out on the one who makes desolate. (Dan. 9:27 NASB)

In the *70 Weeks Prophecy*, Daniel gave his readers (and us) a basic overview of what would take place during the 70th Shabua. In the last chapter, we saw how Jesus would first empower the **New Covenant** by pouring out his Spirit on all believers. We also saw that at the midpoint of the Shabua, Jewish sacrifices and offerings that were occurring in the rebuilt Temple will be taken away and cease. After that, we are told that the Abomination of Desolation will take place. Let's examine why neither the **Historicist Position** nor the **Traditional Futurist Position** are consistent with the biblical record, and why the **Futurist-Spiritual Position** better describes the biblical position.

HISTORICIST POSITION

Historicist opinions on the Abomination in Dan. 9:27 must be consistent with both the Septuagint Greek and the Hebrew text. Most Historicists comment only on the Hebrew text and ignore the Greek because it is extremely challenging to their position.

*On the Temple shall be the abomination of desolations; and at **the** **end of time** an end shall be put to the desolation.* (Dan. 9:27 LXX, emphasis mine)

Obviously, this passage is devastating to Historicist positions. In this passage, it's clear that the Abomination of Desolation spoken of by Jesus in Matt. 24:15 is set up on (Gk.: *epi* meaning "on or upon") the Temple itself. And we also see the desolation lasts **until the end of time**, precluding a fulfillment during the time of Jesus's ministry during his First Coming. Let's examine these points.

Jesus's Reference to the Abomination of Desolation

In the previous chapter, we discussed Matt. 24:3, in which the disciples asked Jesus what the sign of the end of the age would be. What many are unaware of is that this question had its direct roots in the *70 Weeks Prophecy.* First, it was prompted by Jesus's foretelling that not one stone of the Temple would be left upon another (Matt. 24:2). This no doubt brought the *70 Weeks Prophecy* and the destruction of the Temple foretold in Dan. 9:26 to the disciples' minds. We can know this with certainty because they then framed their question using a specific word found in Dan. 9:27.

*The disciples came to Him privately, saying, "Tell us, when will these things happen, and what will be the sign of Your coming, and of the **end** (Gk: **synteleia**) of the age?"* (Matt. 24:3 NASB, emphasis mine)

The Greek word the disciples used for "end" in their question is unusual. It's *synteleia*, meaning "consummation", or "when all the parts come together." It isn't an intermediate end, it's the finale. What was the source of the disciples' use of this word? It's the same Greek word found in Dan. 9:27, translated *"end,"* as in *"end* of time." Therefore, when the disciples asked this question about the "end of the age" in Matt. 24:3, they were in essence asking, "when will the consummation of the age that Daniel spoke of in Dan. 9:27 happen? What will be its sign?"

Jesus responded with a number of events that would happen before the sign. And then he gave them (and us) *the* sign the disciples requested:

> *Therefore, when you* **see** *the abomination of desolation which was spoken of* **through Daniel the prophet***, standing in the holy place [let the reader understand]* (Matt. 24:15 NASB)

Jesus referred the disciples back to Dan. 9:27 *in the Septuagint* and told them that the Abomination of Desolation during the 70th Shabua was *the* sign that the consummation of the age (the consummation of time) was upon them. This cannot be, in any shape or form, an historic event! It is a future event. This proof completely eliminates the **Historicist Position** as a possibility. Let me say it another way — the Historicist Position is impossible.

The Olivet Discourse's *double* reference to the Septuagint version of Dan. 9:27 should be eye-opening to those who hold a Masoretic Text-only (Hebrew-only) position as well. It should be painfully obvious that the disciples and Jesus were referring to the Septuagint text and not the Hebrew text as we know it today. The phrases *"end of time"* (that contains *synteleia*) and "abomination of desolation" are not found in the Masoretic text. Although I don't believe we should trust *only* the Septuagint, this clear set of references demonstrates that we must consider it alongside the Hebrew text and not simply ignore it.

THE TRADITIONAL FUTURIST POSITION

If the Septuagint eliminates the possibility of the **Historicist Position**, the Hebrew Masoretic Text eliminates the **Traditional Futurist Position**.

> *And* **he** *will make a firm covenant with the many for one week, but in the middle of the week* **he** *will put a stop to sacrifice and grain offering; and on the wing of abominations will come* **one who makes desolate**, *even until a complete destruction, one that is decreed, is poured out on the* **one who makes desolate**.
>
> (Dan. 9:27 NASB, emphasis mine)

In the previous chapter, we demonstrated that the "he" in Dan. 9:27 can only be the Messiah, our Lord Jesus. But notice that there are two characters in the verse. *"He,"* whom we've shown is Jesus, and *"one who makes desolate."* This second character can only be the Antichrist. This is even further proof that the "he" who strengthens the Covenant isn't the Antichrist. **The Antichrist can't be both characters**.

146

Drawing of Jesus Cleansing the Temple by Gustave Dore

The *one who makes desolate*, however, is definitely the Antichrist. We know this because Gabriel's words make reference to Isaiah in order to identify him.

> *For **a complete destruction, one that is decreed**, the Lord*
> *God of hosts will execute in the midst of the whole land.*
> (Isa. 10: 23 NASB, emphasis mine)

In Dan. 9:27, we see that the *complete destruction that is decreed* is poured out on the *one who makes desolate* (the Antichrist). In Isa. 10:12, we find out the identity of the Antichrist. There he is referred to as the *"King of Assyria."* Later in verse 17, this is confirmed as the Antichrist because the Holy One of Israel will consume the "briars and thorns" of this king with "fire." That is the complete destruction prophesied in Daniel that happens on the Day of the Lord.

As we demonstrated in Part Four of this book, the *70 Weeks Prophecy* does not support a Roman Antichrist position (in Dan. 9:26). If anything, based on Dan. 9:27 and its link to Isa. 10, it supports an *Antichrist of Middle Eastern descent.*

In the next and final **Part** of the book, we will give suggestions on how Christians should apply this critical prophecy in their everyday lives.

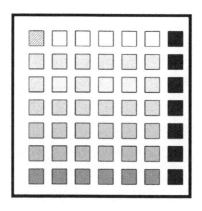

PART SIX:

CONCLUSIONS

Chapter Ten

APPLYING THE 70 WEEKS PROPHECY

Seventy weeks have been decreed for your people and your holy city . . . So you are to know and discern. (Dan. 9:24-25 NASB)

In the *70 Weeks Prophecy*, Daniel gave his readers (and us) a basic overview of what would take place between the decree to rebuild Jerusalem and the consummation of time. He gave us this critical information, history written in advance, so we could apply it in the building up of his Kingdom.

This amazing prophecy allows us to **employ its truth** in a number of different and exciting ways:

- To apply Daniel's prayer as a model prayer,

- To provide a Scriptural tool for evangelizing apostate Jews,

- To demonstrate the timing of the Rapture within the 70th Shabua,

- To identify the region from which the Antichrist will rule,

- To identify the true sign of the consummation of the age, and

- To help identify Jesus's purposes for Christians during the 70th Shabua.

Let's examine these one at a time.

A MODEL PRAYER

In Chapter Three, we discussed Daniel's prayer at some length. We discussed how Daniel identified a promise of God in Scripture and then prayed that promise on behalf of a corporate body, in his case for his nation. We also discussed how Daniel prayed the actual words of God (Daniel quoted Scripture in his prayer) and took a position of humility before the God of the universe. You may want to re-read Chapter Three to refresh your memory about these important aspects of prayer.

We can adopt that same prayer approach. The overwhelming promise of God that may have jumped out at you from this book is the empowering of the Church through the Spirit during the 70th Shabua. Perhaps you may want to begin praying for your church or "the" Church in this way. Pray for the filling of the Spirit, for spiritual gifts of healing and discernment, and for a knowledge of the Word of God. Pray for spiritually-led righteousness to fall upon the Church and for unity among all believers. All these things will be particularly important for the Church during the 70th Shabua that is yet to come.

In terms of praying the promises of God back to him, I suggest also looking up passages about the **New Covenant** or choosing passages about spiritual gifts (1 Cor. 12) and praying using those sections.

If this book is read by 10,000 Christians and all of them begin to pray for this pouring out of the Spirit, what might be the result? Daniel was just one man and look at the result of his prayer. Why not try a prayer like this right now?

JEWISH REPENTANCE

Another wonderful topic to pray about in a "Daniel-Prayer-way" is for the Repentance of the Jews currently living in apostasy, that they will realize that Jesus (Yeshua) is their Messiah, that he was "cut off" for their sins, and that they will come to saving faith.

Although the "countdown to the First Coming" is not something that can be easily used as a tool for evangelism, the *70 Weeks Prophecy* does contain a section that absolutely demonstrates that the Messiah has come.

> *Then after the sixty-two weeks the Messiah will be cut off and have nothing, and the people of the prince who is to come will destroy the city and the sanctuary.* (Dan. 9:26 NASB)

This is a perfect passage to work through with a Jewish friend who is currently denying that Jesus is Messiah. Jews are very aware that the Temple was destroyed in AD 70 and that Jesus was crucified. Discuss this verse with them and show them that according to Daniel's prophecy, the Messiah was killed *prior* to the Temple's destruction. This verse is a challenging, evangelistic verse for unbelieving Jews.

With an understanding of Dan. 9:26, it is difficult, if not impossible, for unbelieving Jews to deny that <u>their Messiah</u> has already come.

Additionally, we can discuss the word "cut off" (*karath*) with our Jewish friends. We can explain how this word is tied to God's fulfilling of the Abrahamic Covenant's blessing to all nations—by sending his Son as the Messiah to die for our sins — thereby paying our sin-debt, which we could never pay ourselves. It is a stunning picture of the compassion and love of our Savior. The *70 Weeks Prophecy* is a beautiful passage where Jew and Gentile can unite in wonder and awe over the plans of redemption of our God and his very Jewish Messiah.

THE 70TH SHABUA DEMONSTRATES PROPER RAPTURE TIMING

You probably never considered that the organization of years in a Shabua would demonstrate Rapture timing. Before we begin to discuss this, lets remind you of the organization of a Shabua.

Figure 10: A Single Shabua

Each Shabua contains six years of toil and a separate, seventh "Year of the Lord," or sabbatical year. This final year is represented by the dark square in the graphic above. This final year of the Shabua is a time when all agricultural work is to cease. This year of rest mimics the Sabbath in a week of days when all work ceases. The 70th Shabua is **no different**. Might the Rapture of the Church occur in this final year? Does the Church "sow and reap" during the first six years of the 70th Shabua by demonstrating the love of Jesus and testifying to an unsaved world about him, and then "rest" in heaven during the final year? Is the Rapture of the Church the final fulfillment of the sabbatical cycle? This division of years during the 70th Shabua is alluded to in Job:

> *He will deliver you from* **six** *troubles; in* **seven** *no evil shall touch you.* (Job 5:19 ESV)

This verse indicates that God will deliver his bond-servants *from* six troubles (possibly years). It also seems to imply the seventh trouble (year) is different; and in that year, evil doesn't even touch the believer. Is that because they are raptured at that point (the seventh year)? I think so.

Those who question this interpretation should study the entire passage (Job 5:11-23). In it, many of the aspects of the 70th Week of Daniel are presented in association with Job 5:19, including war (second seal) famine (third seal), death and destruction (fourth seal), wild beasts (fourth seal), darkness (seventh seal), etc.

In Isaiah, God refers to a one-year period in three separate verses that deal with eschatological prophecies.

> *For the LORD has a day of vengeance, a* **year** *of recompense for the cause of Zion.* (Isa. 34:8 NASB)

> *For the day of vengeance was in My heart, And My* **year** *of redemption has come.* (Isa. 63:4 NASB)

*To proclaim the favorable **year** of the LORD and the day of vengeance of our God; to comfort all who mourn.* (Isa. 61:2 NASB)

All three of these verses equate the day of vengeance (the Day of the Lord) and a one-year period. This year is called a year of redemption, recompense, and favor. First, notice that this year is a "Year of the Lord," the sabbatical year of a seven-year cycle. The three aspects of this year at first seem irreconcilable. How can a single year be all these things? But **God will accomplish a number of different things in this one-year period:**

- Christians will receive God's *favor* and will be raptured into heaven,
- Apostate Jews will receive God's *redemption* and will be saved, and
- The wicked who deserve God's Wrath will receive his *recompense*.

All three purposes refer to the sabbatical year of the 70th Shabua.

Before you write off this explanation, please ask yourself what the meaning is of this final sabbatical year within the 70th Shabua of Daniel if it isn't the timing of the Rapture? Can you find **any other** logical, biblical fulfilment for this final year?

WHERE WILL THE ANTICHRIST ARISE?

As we learned in Chapter Nine, the *70 Week's Prophecy* directly quotes Isa. 10, a passage that refers to an evil, end time ruler known there as the "King of Assyria." Is this proof that the coming "*one who makes desolate*" (the Antichrist) will be of Middle Eastern descent? I believe it is.

THE SIGN OF THE CONSUMMATION OF THE AGE

What is very disturbing to me is that the majority of the Church is expecting the 70th Shabua to begin with a peace treaty between the Antichrist and Israel. As we saw in Chapter Eight, this is not the sign that the 70th Shabua has begun. Now, it's possible a peace treaty may be signed, but it may take place before the 70th Shabua or after it has started.

If a peace treaty that divides the land of Israel is truly signed, it will likely deceive many Christians into believing that the 70th Week has begun. What might be the impact of such a deception? If Christians assume that the 70th Week has started, they may also assume that other events will occur a certain number of years later, and in a particular sequence. If a peace treaty isn't the start of the 70th Shabua, these Christians will be wrong about the timing of their other predictions as well. This may cause them to be disillusioned when events don't happen as they think, and it may be a poor witness for others whom they told that the 70th Week had begun.

As we stated earlier, Jesus never told us to watch for a peace treaty. In fact, Jesus never mentioned a peace treaty. John made no mention of a peace treaty in Revelation, and Paul never mentioned one either. Rather, Jesus told us to watch for the Abomination of Desolation as we mentioned in the previous chapter. This happens at or after the midpoint of the Shabua.

But is there a subtle sign to watch for at the beginning of the 70th Shabua? If this book is correct, there is; but it is one that only believers may notice. Jesus will strengthen the **New Covenant** by pouring out his Spirit on believers. Visions and dreams and healings will vastly increase, even

157

among those who aren't naturally prone to "signs and wonders." Will the Church notice this as a sign? I'm not sure, but it should be evident that the Holy Spirit is giving the Church amazing spiritual gifts at that time.

Additionally, false prophets and false messiahs will say, *"'I am He,'* and, *'The time is near'"* (Luke 21:7 NASB). It is the first sign mentioned in the Olivet Discourse related to the Second Coming of Jesus. So the Church should also be alert for the appearance of one or more false "Messiahs" claiming to be the Lord himself. (Obviously, our true Lord will appear on the clouds as King and Conqueror in spectacular fashion, not as a man on earth.) This is an important distinction for every reader to keep in mind.

However, neither of these last two signs mark the "first day" of the 70th Shabua. There is no specific sign of the first day given in Scripture. No one should begin "counting days or years" based on a "sign" at the beginning of the Shabua. The sign that the consummation of the age is upon us is the Abomination of Desolation at the midpoint, just as Jesus explained to the disciples by quoting the *70 Weeks Prophecy.*

This is the reason that the New and Old Testaments only refer to periods of time such as 1260 days, 42 months, and "time, times, and half a time" (likely to be 3 ½ years). Believers are only to count days and months after the sign of the Abomination of Desolation which occurs half way through the 70th Shabua. They are not to count days after a peace treaty.

SIGNS AND WONDERS

In Matt. 10, Jesus sent out his twelve disciples to minister in Israel. This was a literal event in the first century. However, it is obvious by the end of

Matthew's account that Jesus is discussing the end times as well. He makes a statement that he later quotes in the Olivet Discourse (Matt. 24), and he also mentions his future coming:

> *Brother will betray brother to death, and a father his child; and children will rise up against parents and cause them to be put to death.* **You will be hated by all because of My name, but it is the one who has endured to the end who will be saved.** *But whenever they persecute you in one city, flee to the next; for truly I say to you, you will not finish going through the cities of Israel* **until the Son of Man comes**. (Matt. 10:21-23 NASB, emphasis mine)

It's a matter of disagreement among Christians what portion of Matt. 10 relates to the first century and what portion relates to the 70th Shabua. The reason this is important is that the early portion of Matt. 10 indicates that those Jesus will send out perform incredible signs and wonders:

> *And as you go, preach, saying, "The kingdom of heaven is at hand."* **Heal the sick, raise the dead, cleanse the lepers, cast out demons.** (Matt. 10:7-8 NASB, emphasis mine)

If this is not just something that happened in the first century, but something that will also occur in the 70th Shabua, this is a teaching Christians need to be aware of. Will Jesus give us gifts of the Holy Spirit that include the ability to heal and even raise the dead? Obviously, I don't know, but I strongly suspect he will.

Every Christian should keep this in mind. Our current culture considers that the 70th Shabua will be a time of great danger, with believers forced into hiding. But rather than a time in which Christians are living in bunkers and eating beans, Matt. 10 may indicate that this is a very different lifestyle. Believers may live out ministries much more like the early Church than what we've ever imagined. **This may be the "heroic" future of the Church.**

Now this does not mean that believers won't be persecuted. The Bible is clear that they will be. In fact, most will probably face martyrdom. However, this vision of Christians approaching those times from an *offensive* rather than defensive position needs to be communicated.

The late Ron Morin was a missionary to Central and South America for many years. I met Ron in 2017 on a missionary trip to Guatemala, and I was able to hear his testimony personally. Ron told a mission team I was part of about an amazing experience early in his missionary career. The Spirit of God literally fell on Ron and enabled him to lay-on hands and heal vast numbers of people in South America. Ron told of the sick lining up in theatres and churches for healings, and of the incredible results of cancers being cured, weak hearts being healed, and even tumors shrinking right before the eyes of those who came to see him.

And then, just as quickly as the healing power of the Holy Spirit fell on Ron, it left him. When he inquired of God why he had been given this unique gift, he heard, "As a sign for those who will do this *in the end times.*"

Ron then turned to my group and said, "You will do even greater things than this *in the end times*."

Everyone in our group was quite moved by Ron's testimony. One of my friends had suffered with back problems for years. He asked Ron to pray for him personally. The next day, he woke up without pain and has been pain-free ever since. I wondered if that final healing of my friend was a sign for me as well? Was it a sign to encourage me to share Ron's story and inspire the Church? I think it was.

Will the role of the Church in the 70th Shabua be greater and more empowered than anything we have ever imagined? I think so. It will be the greatest time of testimony in history, why wouldn't it also be the greatest time for the pouring out of the gifts of the Spirit? Miraculous works have traditionally served the purpose of *confirming* a great movement of God.

If you are interested in learning even more about how to prepare for this time, the book ***Simplifying the Rapture*** (Ready for Jesus Publications, 2018) explains other aspects of how to overcome adversity during the 70th Shabua. Pick up a copy and find out for yourself how to prepare for the most challenging and exciting seven-year period in history. You will also be better equipped to share with others about these things.

SUMMARY

Twenty-five-hundred years ago, a righteous man was reading Scripture. What he read encouraged him to pray. The prayer in Dan. 9 resulted in an angelic answer sent from the throne of God himself. That angelic answer was meant for Daniel, of course. But it's meant for us today, as well.

Daniel's prayer in Dan. 9 is an example of prayer at work, and the prophecy that follows it is probably the most exciting prophecy in the Bible, promising the end of sin and everlasting righteousness in the personal presence of Jesus, our Savior. Even the challenging portion of the prophecy (the coming of Antichrist) is filled with blessing — the promise of a strengthening of the **New Covenant** for believers. What an amazing and heroic time lies ahead for those who will live in those days. As the Apostle John wrote at the end of Revelation:

> *He who testifies to these things says, "Surely I am coming quickly."*
> *Amen.* **Even so**, *come, Lord Jesus!* (Rev. 22:20 NKJV, emphasis mine)

My prayer is this: "Even though the time before your return will be challenging, come Lord Jesus. Bring your Kingdom. Bring your Spirit. Empower us to live out the heroic future you have planned for your Church. Amen. **Maranatha!**"

Made in United States
North Haven, CT
13 October 2022